CHOOSING A
COLLEGE MAJOR:
EDUCATION

CHOOSING A COLLEGE MAJOR:

EDUCATION

Harry L. Miller, Ed.D.

Richard Balkin, General Consulting Editor

David McKay Company, Inc.

New York

Library of Congress Cataloging in Publication Data

Miller, Harry L   1920-
Choosing a college major.
Bibliography: p.
Includes index.
1.   Teachers, Training of—United States.
2.   Education—Study and teaching—United States.
I.   Title.
LB715.M54   370'.71'0973   79-10107
ISBN 0-679-50957-7
ISBN 0-679-50958-5 pbk.

1 2 3 4 5 6 7 8 9 10

MANUFACTURED IN THE UNITED STATES OF AMERICA

Contents

CHOOSING A
COLLEGE MAJOR:
EDUCATION

1

Undergraduate Teacher Training: Preliminary Choices

Schools began thousands of years ago, as soon as human life grew so complicated that what children needed to learn could not be taught to them by their families. But, until fairly recent times, it was assumed that anyone who knew something could teach it to someone else, and formal training of teachers started in earnest only a few centuries ago. As a profession, and thus entitled to train its members in the university, teaching is even younger, dating back no earlier than the turn of the present century. The past is worth a brief look, because it created the nature of choices currently open to people who are considering teaching as a career.

The absence of formal settings for the training of teachers did not mean that no training existed. In its oldest form, training was conducted in the way that all skills were then transmitted, by observing and emulating the master teacher. It is a method that should not be belittled, since reformers of teacher education periodically rise up and demand some form of training very close to it. Such teaching apprenticeship was supplemented from time to time by published works of advice and instruction for new teachers, urging them on, warning of pitfalls, and passing on the fruits of experience. One of the most delightful documents of the early Colonial period in America is a series of letters to a friend from a young man who left New England to become a tutor to a family in one of the Southern colonies. Philip Fithian's advice to a friend who was considering taking on a tutoring assignment was typical, and included such sage counsel as this:

> Read over carefully, the lessons in Latin and Greek, in your leisure hours, that the story and Language be fresh in your memory, when you are hearing the respective lessons; for your memory is treacherous, & I am pretty certain it would confound you if you should be accosted by a pert Schoolboy, in the midst of a blunder, with "Physician heal thyself!" You ought likewise to do this with those who are working Figures; probably you may think that because the highest Cypherer is only in decimal arithmetic, is not there fore worth your critical attention to be looking previously into the several Sums. But you are to consider that a sum in the Square-Root, or even in the Single Rule of three direct, is to your Pupils of as great importance, as the most abstruse problem in the Mathematicks to an able artist; & you may lay this down for a Maxim, that they will reckon upon your abilities, according as they find you acquainted and expert in what they themselves are studying.[1]

Formal training of teachers began in the eighteenth century, when the spread of education in western Europe created a demand for teachers. As the first to establish compulsory education in that century, Prussia also became the first to set up teacher-training institutions. These, in turn, created the need for expert knowledge about teaching and learning that could be transmitted by the new institutions, and led to the appointment of university professors of education, responsible for developing that knowledge. This whole network of compulsory education laws, teacher training agencies, and education professors spread to France, England, and, in the nineteenth century, to the United States.

A typical teacher-training institution during the 1800s was the "normal school" (after the French 'L'École Normale'), offering a year or two of formal preparation for young people who, for the most part, had themselves only recently graduated from elementary school. By 1900 most U.S. teachers had at least a bit of such normal school experience before entering the classroom, though what was provided varied widely. The early normal schools all gave students instruction in "how to keep school" as well as a review of what was called (and still is called in some city systems) the "common branches," that is, reading, writing, and arithmetic. Some crammed a good deal more into their two-year program. For example, in the middle of the last century, normal schools in Massachusetts gave courses in algebra, geometry, astronomy, natural philosophy (the sciences), intellectual philosophy, natural history, the history of English literature, United States history, historical geography, and an intensive study of the English language. With that much material to cover in a brief period, courses must have been superficial, but some liberal-arts preparation was clearly important.

As many more people went to high school, normal schools began to demand a high school diploma for entrance, and in response to the lengthening of the span of education, expanded their own offerings to four years and became "teachers' colleges." By 1950 the "normal school" had disappeared, having lasted only a century. Teachers' colleges had an even shorter life; because students who were not interested in teaching careers enrolled in them as a convenient way of getting post-high school educations, most teachers' colleges turned into state colleges and universities. During the same period, already established universities, which in the nineteenth century had offered a few courses in teaching, began developing schools of education, offering programs that ranged from undergraduate preprofessional training to studies leading to the doctor's degree.

Today, as an end result of these developments, 80 percent of all four-year colleges operate some kind of teacher training program, at fourteen hundred different institutions. At most of them students interested in teaching either at the elementary or at the high school level can take the courses they must have to get a teaching certificate granted by one of the state departments of education. At one extreme are small, liberal-arts colleges, which offer courses in education leading to a teaching certificate, as a sort of added service for their regular undergraduate students. The courses are taught by one or two faculty members at most. At the other extreme are large uni-

3

versities, with separate schools of education having faculties of two hundred to three hundred instructors.

The rest of this introductory chapter is devoted to describing the most important areas of choice open to students, not just in selecting a training program but in selecting a college that offers the kind of program they want.

What Teaching Level?

This is possibly the most important decision to be made, and one that some fortunate students do not have to agonize over. But for others it is by no means as easy a decision as it was when women generally selected elementary teaching and men chose high school. Although the trend has only recently begun to show up in statistical studies, many college teachers report an increased interest among male education students in working with younger children, and a greater willingness among women to consider less traditional school roles for women.

The numbers of levels have themselves increased. The old pattern of eight elementary years followed by four years of high school changed a generation ago into a new tradition of 6-3-3, with the junior high school inserted in the middle to siphon off youngsters from both of the other schools during the most turbulent years of early adolescence. More recently, some larger cities have created "middle schools," which, in a variety of patterns, separate the upper grades of the elementary school from the lower ones. The lower grades in turn have come to be be thought of as "early childhood."

Each of these ways of organizing the twelve years of American schooling attempts to deal with special problems and provides at least a partial solution, while creating new problems along the way. For the most part, however, the teacher training programs in the colleges simply kept their old forms, preparing students either for K-6 (kindergarten through sixth grade), or for secondary school (both junior and senior high school). The elementary program has added on nursery school at the lower end and become N-6 in most places; otherwise little has changed. What may seem to be a resistance to change really is not; colleges and universities must pay careful attention to the "levels" that the states license their students to teach, and state authorities are reluctant to change their licensing rules.

Making the choice between the two major types of programs is much more than a matter of deciding the period of childhood with which you prefer to work. The demands of the programs differ so greatly that students, in selecting one of them, make some very serious decisions about the rest of their college careers. Here is a typical elementary teaching sequence of courses, based on a random check of twenty-five college catalogs (the content of these courses will be examined in detail in the next chapter):

Introduction to Education	3 credits
Social (or historical, or philosophical) *Foundations of Education* (In some sequences these social foundations courses may require 6 credits, but include the introductory course)	3
Child Development	3
Human Learning and Classroom Dynamics (In some colleges the above two courses are referred to as Psychological Foundations)	3
Curriculum and Teaching Methods in the Elementary School (Wide variation exists in the mix of these courses; see Chapter 3)	9–15
Student Teaching in the Elementary School	7–12

This sequence of typical courses is a bare-bones minimum. At some schools students are required to take the maximum of the ranges shown, as well as a number of courses (art, music, or physical education, for example) in other departments, for as many as sixty credits. This is close to half the total credits in most undergraduate programs. Some states have, further, responded to such problems as reading difficulties or drug addiction among children by requiring special courses in re-

5

medial reading instruction or in the causes and treatment of addiction.

Secondary education sequences, in contrast, are far more academically demanding, but much less so professionally. Preparation for future high school teachers generally requires that students choose a major and minor in fields appropriate to high school licensing requirements (English, math, science, social studies, etc.), and a fairly modest number of education courses, as in the following typical pattern:

Social (or historical, or philosophical) *Foundations*	3 credits
Psychological Foundations (Here the child development course focuses on the adolescent years)	6
Curriculum, organization, and administration of the high school	4–6
Student teaching	5–7

The number of professional credits in this case seldom adds up to more than twenty or twenty-one; most of the intensive preparation of future secondary school teachers is in the subject matter areas they will teach. In higher education the shift in emphasis continues so that the training of college instructors focuses exclusively on mastering a field of study and no time at all—unfortunately—is spent on the process of teaching.

Students often describe the choice between the elementary and secondary sequence as depending on whether one tends to be more interested in and enthusiastic about teaching itself, or about a subject field. Clearly, the meaning of the college years as a whole should be considered. For some young people they are the road that must be traveled directly to a desired career, in which case the heavy emphasis on professional course work in the elementary sequence is not a serious drawback. Others view college at least partly as an opportunity to explore a number of intellectual and unknown paths that life might never encourage them to sample later. For them, an undergraduate professional preparation that more easily fits into a regular academic program might be preferable.

What Kind of College?

Because so many students are interested in teaching, it would be very difficult to operate any general undergraduate college program without offering some work in education—enough, as earlier noted, to provide students with an opportunity to get a teacher's license after graduation. Programs are plentiful, and in many parts of the country they are in competition with one another for students. If students are lucky enough to be able to choose their college, they can try to match the college to some of their own likes and dislikes, as well as to available career opportunities.

For example: high school trainees—and even the elementary school trainees taking a large number of college credits in the professional field—will spend more than half of their time in liberal-arts courses. In the large universities, and particularly in those with a great deal of academic prestige, the fact that students are enrolled in a preprofessional training sequence is likely to be ignored, and any connection between liberal-arts content and the field of education overlooked. If a course in urban affairs taken in the sociology department has something important to say for professionals in education (and it usually does), students generally will have to see the connection themselves. Survey courses in literature are unlikely to provide very much help to future elementary school teachers interested in children's stories, though most English departments do offer a course in children's literature.

The low-man-on-the-totem-pole status of teacher education in many such universities has other effects as well. Members of the faculty are very well aware of the fact that their promotion and salary depend on their activity as scholars—doing research in their fields, and publishing the results in books and journals. They are inclined as a result to be less interested than they might in their own teaching, or in the practical skills involved in teaching as a profession. Even when experienced teachers in the public schools are brought on to university faculties they sometimes have trouble keeping their attention focused on the needs of the professional sequence, because there is a great deal of pressure on them to devote time to research and writing.

All of these pressures have a real impact on undergraduate

education majors at large universities. They often get no real sense of the profession until they are out in the schools during student teaching (though in very recent years contact with the field has been much on the increase in ways that a later chapter will describe). Those students who are academically very able may be actively discouraged from pursuing professional goals in education and urged instead to concentrate on some academic field.

Many of these same problems may be found in a different form in the small liberal-arts colleges that provide some service courses for their students interested in teacher certification, but do not consider them part of their central mission. Although it is difficult to escape these drawbacks in *any* collegiate setting, the chances of avoiding them are probably greatest in well-established schools of education with large faculties that include many professors trained in academic fields but professionally committed to making the application of these fields to teaching. Such faculties have artists interested in children's artistic expression, well-trained scientists working on improving high school science instruction, urban sociologists attempting to increase our understanding of city schools and their difficulties.

But, as with the choice between elementary and secondary school teaching, not all students want to be so immersed in the study of education. So the choice of a college should also begin with an estimate of how much professional commitment the student feels.

Those who feel:

> . . . a strong commitment to a long-term teaching career
> . . . a wish to identify with the profession and with those who are also strongly committed to it
> . . . a need for close contact with professionals who can act as professional role models

might try to enrol in a large school of education within a university, as described above.

Those who feel:

> . . . a need to explore a number of fields before making a final commitment to a profession

... an interest in education as a wider field beyond that of the public school

... a strong commitment to some academic field of study

might be quite content with a setting in which the liberal arts dominate the undergraduate professional programs.

Which Academic Minors?

Students preparing to teach in junior or senior high schools must, of course, major in a discipline related to the field they intend to teach. High school requirements have loosened up a great deal in recent years, and high school students may have a wide array of courses from which to choose, but secondary teaching licenses are still granted in a fairly limited number of fields. English, science, social studies, foreign languages, and health and physical education have been the standard areas for some time and will probably remain so.

A college minor to go along with a secondary major may be an easy choice to make; often it might be another subject within the same academic area: a biology minor for a physics major, speech or communications along with English literature, sociology with a major in history, and so on. But physical education majors are often encouraged to build some strength in a solid academic field; in a small school they might have to flesh out their athletic activities with some periods in a regular classroom. Liberal-arts majors with a personal need for variety, or with a desire to build some flexibility into their later careers, might deliberately choose a minor in a field quite different from that of their major, even if to do so they have to elect a double minor.

Choice of a minor is much less clear-cut for those preparing to teach the elementary grades, and college faculty who counsel these students often get the impression that they devote less serious thought to the matter, which is a pity. The attitude is reasonable enough, to be sure, since the elementary teacher is usually responsible for all of the major subject areas of the lower grades and feels the need to be somewhat competent in all of them. But, as noted earlier, future elementary teachers spend so much time in professional courses that their minor gives them their only opportunity to deal with an academic subject in some depth, and it makes sense for them to think carefully about what that subject should be.

Their most common choice is a minor in psychology, with sociology probably taking second place. The reasoning behind the popularity of psychology is clear: the subject matter taught in the lower grades, students argue, never gets very complicated, so the real need of the teacher is for knowledge of how to motivate children and how to help them learn—therefore psychology. A somewhat similar argument is followed to justify sociology: children's motivation in school very much depends on background factors that are part of family, ethnic group, and community; the more that teachers know about these, the more likely it is that they will be able to understand and motivate the child.

There is nothing seriously wrong with this thinking, and students who are, in addition, interested in one of these fields would be well advised to adopt one of these as a minor. But those who expect to find in either academic psychology or in sociology practical and concrete help in deciding what to do in the elementary school classroom are bound to be disappointed. Neither of these sciences is sufficiently advanced to be able to predict with any confidence the behavior of either adults or children, although they can provide some very interesting and useful explanations for behavior after the fact. Teachers are generally more interested in prediction than in explanation. Moreover, the human or social problems that interest a college instructor in these fields may not have much bearing on the problems of the classroom.

There are alternatives to these fairly obvious choices for minors. One is to try for depth in one of the important content areas of the elementary grades by taking a minor in English, or in one of the natural sciences, such as botany or geology, that tend to fascinate young children. Or, a talent for music or art should encourage students possessing the gift to consider a minor leading to an elementary school specialization in the field. Such positions are becoming reasonably common around the country.

"Standard" or "Alternative" Program?

Until the last ten years or so, teacher preparation programs at the undergraduate college level were very much standardized; although the number of credits required for various parts of the program differed from college to college, the sequence of courses itself was pretty much the same, and the lecture-discussion format within the regular classroom was the common practice.

There has recently been a great deal of experimentation with new forms of college training for teachers-to-be. The federal Office of Education (part of HEW) has contributed funds to support tryouts of many new ideas, so programs that are intended as "alternative" ways of educating teachers may be found across the country, often in colleges and universities where one would least expect to find them. A few specific programs of this kind will be described in detail in a later chapter; here, as part of a discussion of questions that students might ask themselves in the early stages of considering a college career, is a broad look at the general trends.

Early In-School Training

By far the most important trend in teacher education is the recent heavy emphasis on getting students into the schools as early as possible. Because providing field experiences is usually much more expensive than operating the normal classroom, most earlier teacher preparation programs tended to put those experiences off until students reach the "student teaching" course at the end of the entire sequence. Almost all programs of any size now do a great deal more than that, beginning with the assignment of students as early as the freshman year to do some tutoring of young children who need remedial work. As future teachers get further along in the sequence and more familiar with the professional side of public schools, they may act at times as teacher's aides or assume for a half hour or so teaching responsibilities for small groups of children. Some programs have moved far beyond these still-limited field experiences, making the elementary or high school the center of the four-year college experience, with education faculty coming into the field to teach their courses on site.

Exploring the Community

A number of special teacher-training programs place a major emphasis not only on school-based field experience but on a thorough exploration of the community from which the children come. In such programs students might find themselves attending, and writing papers about, school-board meetings, parents' association committee sessions, and other community activities that might not even have a direct connection with the school.

Ethnic Focus

Some teacher preparation sequences, in universities that send many of their graduates into the schools of the larger cities, have developed a special focus on the ethnic and cultural variety that may increasingly be found in urban America. Students are encouraged to develop positive attitudes toward children from different cultural backgrounds, and to understand and take into account in the classroom the great variety of ethnic groups in the U.S. communities.

"Do-It-Yourself"

Several innovative programs have moved a very considerable distance toward having students take the responsibility for their own learning. Students are provided with clear statements of the teaching skills they must learn in order to complete the program, and with carefully developed materials that they can use without much faculty help, working on their own. When students think they have mastered a given skill area, they can arrange to be tested in it. Failure to attain the required level of mastery brings on no crisis; it is merely a signal that the student needs to get some more practice, or take another try at understanding.

Whether or not one of these new approaches is your particular cup of tea obviously depends on you. If you are attracted by novel and experimental situations, you will find in the Appendix a listing of where some of the more interesting innovations may be found.

How Selective Are Teacher-Training Programs?

Students entering college in the late 1970s and early 1980s may find themselves in the midst of a change to higher standards in the selection and retention of enrollees in teacher preparation programs. Although for many years there has been a good deal of talk about setting standards for entry into the profession, a recent survey has found that colleges and universities actually are not very selective at all. Most institutions reject fewer than 10 percent of the teacher education applicants; and, although almost all teacher preparation programs set some standards for retaining students in the program, few students in the past have been eliminated.

The reason why these standards have generally been so low is not hard to find. During the 1960s a serious shortage of teachers throughout the country, particularly in the larger cities, put a great deal of pressure on teacher training programs to graduate as many licensed teachers as possible. Any large-scale effort to impose tough standards of either selection or retention would have been viewed by school systems as an unfriendly act.

Because many of the larger-than-usual number of children who were born in the late 1940s and 1950s worked their way through elementary and high school, the shortage of teachers finally ended in the early 1970s. Many teacher-educators thought that the time had come to set standards for the profession by tightening up on the screening procedures by which students were admitted to programs. Not so, however, because an unexpected and very sudden drop in teacher education students posed new problems for the colleges, whose faculties were still suitable in size for the earlier larger number of students.

As these staffing problems recede, and students and faculty begin to come into balance again, the question of standards comes up for reconsideration in a number of institutions. Students might well confront one or another of the following possible developments:

Grades Plus Ability

Selection procedures in the past have usually involved mainly the application of *academic* standards, and not very high ones at that. One fairly common requirement is that education students maintain at least a 2.0 (C) average as freshmen in order to be admitted into the teaching sequence. Colleges of education, which admit students into the program as freshmen, usually apply an equivalent standard on the high school grade point average. Many educators are now calling for additional evidence of capability: success in laboratory teaching experiences, a demonstration of interest in and aptitude for teaching, and appropriate personality characteristics.

More Counseling

During the sequence itself, it is suggested, students should be given much more interviewing and counseling, and more comprehensive records should be kept on their progress and their demonstrated capabilities. The question of whether a student should be retained in the program is likely to be addressed much more systematically and involve more of the faculty and administration at various checkpoints.

Flexibility

In the long run, the selection process that leads to admission into the teacher-training program may be left quite flexible and the hurdles kept deliberately low, with effort put into improving the process by which students are retained or counseled out of the program. The retention process will probably take the form of careful testing of students' performance before they are allowed to exit with the proper credentials; in effect, students will have an "exit visa" stamped with the college's guarantee that the bearer has demonstrated mastery of a specific number of teaching competencies.

What Kind of Commitment?

Finally, in choosing a college, a major, or a career, students considering undergraduate preparation for teaching might examine their motivation for entering on that career. As the results of the survey reported in Table 1 indicate,[2] a variety of motives come into play for different people who enter the profession. Those who have had a lot of contact with young people in teacher preparation programs might suspect a tendency among the teachers reporting here to choose the more

Table 1. Reasons Given by Teachers for Choosing Teaching as a Career

Consideration in Choosing Teaching as Career	All reporting	Men	Women	Elementary	Secondary
Number of teachers reporting	2,316	723	1,593	1,218	1,098
Desire to work with young people	34%	33%	35%	39%	29%
Opportunity for rendering important service	28	25	29	32	23
Interest in a subject-matter field	14	19	11	5	23
A tradition in my family	6	3	8	8	5
Example set by a favorite teacher	6	5	6	5	7
Job security	6	8	5	6	6
Financial rewards	2	.6	2	2	1
Easiest preparation program in college	1	2	.8	1.2	.9
Unsuccessful in another line of work	.4	1	.1	.1	.7
Stopgap until marriage	.3	—	.4	.3	.3
Other reason	3	4	2	3	3

noble-sounding motives. It is important to realize that such socially approved motives as "an opportunity for rendering important service" do not necessarily have to be on the top of everyone's priority list.

People who choose to enter one of the teaching professions ought to have some interest in serving others, to be sure, and in the field of teaching one hopes that teachers-to-be like to work with children. But many educators would have been pleased if a greater number of those in the survey had indicated a real enthusiasm for a subject-matter field.

There has been a good deal of argument over the years about whether teaching is a genuine profession, or just a high-level craft. Any number of ideas have been advanced as a basis for arguing that teaching is a profession, but it is possible that the attitudes of those practicing a profession say more about whether or not they are professionals than does mere membership in a particular occupation. It is this kind of commitment that Herbert Thelen describes so well:

> Do you remember the fine old story about the two brick-layers? They were asked "What are you doing?" One replied, "I am laying bricks." The other said, "I am building a cathedral." The first man is a tradesman; the second has the soul of an artist or professional. The difference is in the meaning of the activity. It is not in how expertly or skillfully the bricklayers daub mortar onto each brick; it is not in how much information they have about the job; it is not in their loyalty to the boss; it is not in their familarity with other constructions. It is in how they savor and feel about what they are doing, in their sensing of relationships between their work and that of others, in their appreciation of poten-tialities, in their sense of form, in their need for and enjoy-ment of significance, in their identification of self with ci il-ized aspirations, in their whole outlook on life.[3]

NOTES

1 *Journal and Letters of Philip Vickers Fithian, 1773–1774*, quoted in S. Alexander Rippa, *Educational Ideas in America* (New York: David McKay Company, 1969), p. 37.
2 National Education Association, *The American Public School Teacher* (Washington, D.C.: NEA Publications, 1967), p. 59. Figures have been rounded.
3 Herbert Thelen, "Profession, Anyone?", *New Perspectives in Teacher Education* (San Francisco: Jossey-Bass Publishers, 1973), p. 198.

2

The Foundations of Education

The part of the education sequence usually referred to as the foundations courses comes, appropriately enough, early in the program. A general introductory course may be offered separately, or as part of one of the courses in the foundations, which consist of:

(a) *psychological foundations,* a group of courses that deals with what we know about how children grow and develop, how they learn, and how they interact with one another in group settings such as the classroom;

(b) *social foundations,* a much more varied group of courses that show how the schools relate to their societies: the historical circumstances that created modern school systems, conflicts about what social purposes the schools should serve, and how the school experiences of different social groups influence the lives of the members of those groups.

The courses in this segment are primarily academic courses (that is, more theoretical than practical), and resemble the liberal-arts courses that are part of the general college experience. This similarity is usually found in the subject matter of the foundations courses—although there has been some recent movement to make it relate more sharply to the practical and concrete problems of school professionals—as well as in what is required of the student.

The reason for the similarity just noted is easy enough to

account for: educational foundations courses, whatever else they may be, are attempts to apply concepts from academic fields, such as history, philosophy, and sociology, to the problems of the schools. Because the foundations courses inhabit a not very well-defined position between those fields and the professional preparation program devoted to training teachers, they are the focus for a considerable amount of administrative and departmental conflict. Every once in a while in most colleges someone raises the question of whether it might not be better all around for the psychology department to teach the educational psychology courses, the history department to take over historical foundations, and so on. To which the education faculty is apt to reply that these departments are too interested in theory to pay much attention to the practical problems that concern future teachers, and that a special educational breed of psychologists, and historian, and sociologist, is needed.

Students are seldom much affected by these faculty disagreements, though the courses they take may become more, or less, academic as a result. Some education majors are so focused on getting prepared for the classrooms they will later take over as teachers that they consider the foundations requirements a distraction from their real work of preparation. But, if teaching is to be considered a profession, teachers must have some grasp of the theoretical basis of the skills they practice in the classroom. To learn how to teach children to read is necessary for students who will later teach in the third grade, but it is also important for them to know why some groups of people in the society disagree about how important it is for children to learn to read at all, and why some groups of children learn to read much less well than others.

Introduction to Teaching

When such a course is offered separately it is often called the "entry course," and consists of a broad survey of teaching as a profession and of the school as an institution, giving these topics much more detailed attention than is possible in a typical social foundations course.

Later chapters in this book offer some good examples of the

subject matter covered in such a course: Chapter 8 on teaching as a career, Chapter 9 on life in school, and Chapter 10 on career opportunities. Other topics often included in an introduction to teaching course are described under the "social foundations" heading later in this chapter; they include such issues as conflicts over the goals of instruction, different versions of the ideal teacher, and the problems of teaching children of new immigrant groups.

The Psychological Foundations

Of all the course work that deals with background and theory of education, the psychologically based material is usually seen by students as closest to their first interest: the classroom role of the teacher. Teachers spend most of their time, after all, working with children of various ages and at differing periods of development. Courses that explore how children grow and develop, that outline the opportunities and problems of particular stages of development, that review what is known about learning in general and human learning in particular, and that examine the general problems of dealing with groups of children in a classroom setting, are bound to interest future teachers.

The subject matter of educational psychology covers a wide range of topics and problems. One way of putting them into some kind of order is first to divide them roughly into three major concerns: the *learner*, the *learning process*, and the *learning situation*. Within those broad areas, the following discussion of the content of the field touches on some, though by no means all, of the important subjects that students are likely to meet.

The Content of the Psychological Foundations

The Learner. The focus usually remains on the first of the three concerns, the learner, for at least a full semester, and, in programs that require more than a year of educational psychology, for as long as two semesters. The growth of children in all its aspects has been closely studied since the beginning of this century; it is an enterprise that has joined the efforts of pediatricians with those of psychologists and psychiatrists, as well as educators.

The degree to which the birth and very early life of the infant is dealt with in these courses tends to vary a good deal, as opinions differ on the importance of the events of this earliest stage. Some texts provide considerable coverage of what is known about prenatal influences on the child, the influence of inheritance on the physical and mental characteristics of the child, and childbirth itself. In recent years, a very heavy emphasis in the field as a whole on the importance of environmental influences, and on the immediate living situation of the individual child at any stage, has tended to decrease the attention given to genetics and to such early events as birth. The change reflects only one episode of an ongoing crucial and complicated twentieth-century dispute in the social sciences, which is sometimes called the nature/nurture controversy.

The period of growth from birth to entrance into school at about the age of five is, again, given varying degrees of emphasis, depending on how much attention a particular program has decided to give to educational psychology as a whole. Students might find themselves spending a good deal of time on development during infancy, with detailed attention given to the stages of growth in physical competence, what the field calls "psychomotor development" (focusing the eyes, sitting up, creeping, crawling, walking, toilet training, and so on). The course might then move on to consider in some detail the toddler stage, with the beginnings of language and the development of self-awareness and early moves toward independence, then to the preschool child's mastery of language.

More important than the mere description of the processes and actions that accompany these stages of growth—and others that follow the child through the middle years of childhood (the elementary school years) and then into adolescence—are the fascinating attempts the field has made to organize them into a framework that helps students, and later, teachers, understand the relation between one stage and another.

One such framework, or theory, deals with the aspect of development that psychologists call "cognitive," that is, activities that involve perceiving, thinking, or problem-solving. The person mainly responsible for the current generally accepted theory is Jean Piaget, the Swiss psychologist who has for many years been setting cognitive tasks for children to do, watching them while they perform, then talking with them about what they did. One of his typical experiments involves pouring all the water from a squat, wide glass into a tall, thin glass, in which, of course, its level is much higher. Before a specific stage of development very young children will always report that the tall, thin glass "has more water in it"; no amount of explanation will serve to convince them of the truth of the matter. After a new developmental stage has been achieved, however, children do not need the explanation—they understand immediately that the same amount of water is involved.

Piaget thus sees cognitive development as a well-defined series of stages; children's ability to learn depends on the stage they happen to be in (their "readiness"), as well as their experience in the preceding stages. Piaget very much emphasizes the importance of having young children learn directly through their senses (touching, seeing, hearing, etc.) instead of through reading or through explanation by an adult. He also argues that there is little use in trying to teach children some specific skill or insight until they have reached the appropriate developmental stage for it, a conclusion that is not acceptable to some educators interested in cognitive training for very young pre-school children.

Children also move through more or less clearly defined stages of emotional growth; such development is "affective," in contrast to "cognitive." One of the most interesting and currently influential theories of this aspect of development was suggested by Erik Erikson. According to Erikson, children must face a series of emotional conflicts as they grow, conflicts that he calls "psychosocial crises." Before children can move confidently on to the next stage of emotional development, they must solve the crisis of the stage they are in.

So, the infant, in a world that is a "booming, buzzing confusion," must solve the conflict between trusting or not trusting the mother to meet its most basic needs for food and security. In a later stage that occurs during the year or so before entering school, children are able to take more initiative in deciding on their own activities. They may either develop that initiative, or feel guilty about doing things independently instead of depending on the adults of the family. Still much later, young adults go through a stage in which they deal with learning how to maintain closeness with other people, in friendship as well as in sexual relationships, or choose to steer clear of such intimacy and remain isolated. Erikson has described eight stages of these kinds, from infancy to mature age, and they are very illuminating tools for all adults who must work with children.

The Learning Process. In this second area, the psychological foundations focus on the variety of ways, and the many different settings, in which children learn.

Most of the learning that children acquire happens outside of school, and to a remarkable degree, the most important learning has taken place by the time they arrive in school. Education students are likely to find a considerable emphasis in the foundations work on the role of the family in setting the stage for school learning through what has been called "the hidden curriculum" of the home. Within the family children learn to like or dislike the kinds of tasks that the school will later require them to do, learn how to make use of adult help in meeting problems, learn habits of concentration and the ability to accept limits on one's own freedom in pursuit of some longer-term goals, and so on. The family has a very considerable influence, then, on whether the children are "teachable" when they arrive in school for the first time. Family pressures on, or support for, children in succeeding years of their school careers also considerably influence later school success. The role and impact of other out-of-school "teachers" of growing children are also examined: their peers, adults they meet in the neighborhood, and so on.

Next to the study of the stages of child development, however, the most important part of educational psychology is likely to be learning theory. Depending on the university, and on whether a student takes this course work in an education division or a department of psychology, the treatment of this crucial subject can involve either a highly technical study of a number of attempts at building a theory of learning—based firmly on very careful laboratory experimentation—or, at the other extreme, views of learning that depend on particular assumptions about human beings. An example of this latter type of approach sees learning as a natural and normal human activity that does not have to be artificially stimulated by the schools, especially if they permit children to choose their own learning goals. Whichever of these theoretical approaches are favored, however, students are apt to confront an unfamiliar vocabulary: operant conditioning, phenomenology, Gestalt, goal gradients, and similar technical terms, and should be prepared for the shock.

The Learning Situation. The focus, in this third area, is on the classroom and how it should be structured. Where the different approaches to psychology stand on this issue depends, of course, on the learning theory preferred. Those who believe that children's learning is largely influenced by how and when their behavior (cognitive or social) is rewarded emphasize the teacher's dominant role in the classroom. Those who are more impressed by the *natural* quality of children's learning, when learners are engaged in moving toward their own goals, call for a much more flexible and open learning environment, with the teacher acting as a stage-setter instead of the person in command. Chances are that both approaches will be described in any text students are asked to use in these courses, because text publishers want to ensure the broadest market for their books, and because instructors want to present important sides of the conflict fairly. But there *is* a good deal of conflict about these matters, and students would be well advised to enter the study of educational psychology with minds as open to the debate as they can manage.

The Psychology of the Adolescent

The adolescent stage of growth, beginning approximately at the middle of junior high school, give or take a few years for individual youngsters, is an enormously important and complicated stage in itself. Teachers of basic courses in educational psychology spend a good deal of time complaining to each other about the problem of trying to fit infancy, childhood, and adolescence into the same course, and they usually agree that one end or the other tends to be neglected.

A student enrolled in a program combining elementary and

secondary majors in its psychological foundations course may find that the adolescent period is skimpily covered. In that case, he or she should seriously consider taking a course in adolescent psychology as an elective.

A study of the problems of adolescent boys and girls can be particularly interesting and rewarding to young people, who are just emerging from that stage of development themselves and assuming adult status. Consider these common topics in such a course: the physical changes that for several years give adolescents little security in their own sense of self; powerful new emotions, difficult to understand and to control; frustration with the prolonged postponement of adult status, and uncertainty about the adult roles that must sooner or later be undertaken; the awkwardness and self-consciousness of the adolescent years, and the search for a meaningful identity.

Two Current Issues in Educational Psychology

Some of the problems that a course in educational psychology deals with involve issues of growth in the very complicated context of family and society. The entire education profession has been trying for years to grapple with the differences between minority-group children and mainstream (middle-class white) children in mastering the tasks set for them by the schools. Somewhere around the third grade many minority children begin to fall behind the learning gains of the average child; only some manage to catch up by the end of high school.

One psychological explanation (there are many others) of the problem runs this way: Learning the things that schools ask us to learn requires a complicated array of cognitive abilities, most of which we acquire in infancy and early childhood. If, because families and neighborhoods do not provide enough stimulation for the growing infant, the opportunity to master these abilities at the proper time is missed, children find it much more difficult to do so later in life.

If this theory is correct, it follows that providing the right kinds of cognitive stimulation in early infancy should solve the problem. A number of federally and state-funded experimental programs attempting to do just that have been set up over the past decade and have, unfortunately, created more

25

arguments than they have settled. Now the problem is to decide, on the basis of experimental finding, whether programs prove that the theory is correct—a difficult, if fascinating, task.

A question much closer to the classroom is: What limits should be set on children's behavior, and how should they be imposed? The following brief discussion of that problem, from a major textbook in educational psychology, will also serve as an example of the writing style and vocabulary level students are likely to encounter in these courses:[1]

> One of the perplexing characteristics of children, particularly, during the preadolescent period, is their need, on the one hand, to have someone set limits for their behavior and, on the other, to test or challenge the very limits that have been set. We often find ourselves drawn into a kind of trap because of these ambiguous and often contradictory motives. Some adults, when confronted by complaints of children that limitations on their behavior are too severe, react by doing away with all or most limits. Thereupon they are appalled when children respond to this greater freedom by actually worsening their behavior and blaming the adult in charge for what has gone wrong. On the other hand, adults who attempt to deal with this ambiguous situation by being severe, restrictive, and punitive cannot understand why children are so apathetic and why the behavior of some children actually becomes worse.
>
> Such experiences show that the behavior of children cannot be handled on an "all-or-none" basis. The effective teacher is one who can allow children freedom to develop naturally and spontaneously, but who can also set limits to their behavior at appropriate times. The better the morale of the group and the better the learning situation, the less need there should be to invoke limits.

What Goes on in the Classroom

Much of classroom activity in this area is likely to resemble the typical liberal-arts classroom in the college: some lecture, group discussion of the readings, and so on. As the emphasis shifts to the practical application of psychological theories and research, however, student participation in class may take on quite a distinctive cast.

For example, during the study of two key topics in psychological foundations—growth and development, and classroom dynamics—many instructors put a great deal of emphasis on having students observe children's behavior closely. Such assignments might include recording observations of a young child in the student's family, or an individual pupil in a classroom in which the student is observing and tutoring, or interviewing an adolescent brother or sister. Some time in class is usually devoted to reporting on and discussing these observations, and relating them to generalizations in the texts and lectures. Most education faculties consider this kind of activity to be of great importance, because it provides future teachers with practice in child study, one of the major tasks that they will later take on in the school setting.

A second related activity concerns class discussions of individual case studies of children, presented either in the text or by the instructor. Students are usually given an opportunity to study the case by themselves, and to answer some questions about the child the case describes, before discussion is begun. Such discussions may start with a request for a variety of interpretations of a particular phase of development, or a behavior problem, and then move to a consideration of what evidence there is in the case write-up that would support the interpretation offered. This approach can provide very useful training not only for future teachers but for a wide range of professional roles in the human-services field.

Also, some instructors are particularly interested in the group dynamics of the classroom, and often use class time for group exercises aimed at giving students vivid insight into the internal forces that teachers must be aware of in their classroom groups. For example, when groups work at a task that has not been clearly explained, group members tend to display "out-of-field" behavior: horseplay, withdrawal, conversation about after-school activities, and the like. In order to demonstrate this tendency the college instructor might break the class ino two groups, one given well-defined, clear instructions for a group activity, the other given vague and ambiguous instructions. At the end of fifteen or twenty minutes, the instructor stops the activity and asks members of the class to compare the behavior of the two groups, and find an explanation for the differences.

This kind of classroom exercise is sometimes referred to as "experiential learning," because it creates a real experience whose point must be puzzled out in the same way that we learn from our life experience.

The Social Foundations

This part of the foundations area uses the tools and ideas of a number of fields to help students understand some recurrent problems in education. To call them problems is really misleading, because it suggests that some day they might be solved, or settled. Each society, in fact, finds somewhat different answers to them, and shifts to new answers at different times. Some of the most significant of these hardy perennials are:

> Of all the many goals that education can have, which ones shall we select to emphasize?
>
> Who shall teach our young, and what is the best model of the teacher?
>
> Who shall be educated, and if all children be included, shall the goals be different for various groups of them?
>
> What should be taught in schools, and for how long, and how intensely?
>
> Who shall control the schools, and who should decide how much of society's resources shall be used for education?

The Content of Social Foundations Courses

It is possible to address questions of the kind just mentioned in a course that is organized around them, with history, philosophy, and the social sciences brought to bear on them together. As is more often the case, however, one section of a course, or an entire course, may be devoted to the historical foundations, another to the philosophical, and so on, depending on the specific department's preference. Although the ways in which the fields are put together are too different to yield a "typical" pattern, the topics explored are fairly standard.

Historical. The history of education may still, in a minority of college programs, include the entire Western world, beginning with the glory that was Greece and proceeding majestically to the present. In U.S. universities it has tended to narrow to the story of the development of our school system during the three-and-a-half centuries since the founding of the English colonies. Within this span rather less attention is paid to the Colonial period and more to the movements and ideas that began with the establishment of mass, publicly supported schools in the early part of the nineteenth century.

A good course in the historical foundations will describe the development over time of all the "hardy perennial" problems just discussed. It will describe, for example, how the mainly religious goals of the church-run schools of our Colonial period became heavily vocational, and later became concerned with personal and individual development. It will also discuss the shift in instructional patterns in some public schools, from 150 years ago when classrooms were run like army regiments, with all the children at attention, to modern open-space settings in which small groups or single individual busy themselves at diverse tasks on their own. The course might deal at length with the gradual extension of public schooling to new groups of children, girls as well as boys, blacks as well as whites, American Indian children in the West, and whites in isolated rural mountain areas.

Philosophical. These foundations courses, or parts of courses, differ sharply from the content of academic philosophy. In recent years, philosophy has come to emphasize the language in which ideas are communicated rather than the values of the ideas themselves or their application to the everyday life of humans living in society. Some courses in the philosophy of education have followed this trend; they spend a good deal of time on rather abstract analysis of ideas related to education: what do we really mean, for example, when we say that a student has "learned" something?

Most foundations courses in this area, however, focus their attention on the differences between various ideas about education, and the conflicts in the human values involved in these

29

ideas. One of the ways in which we demonstrate our educational values, for example, is in our beliefs about what the schools should teach—their curriculum. It is all very well for the historian to point out that U.S. school systems go through periods of great concern about "getting back to the basics" (meaning reading, writing, and arithmetic); that observation shows merely that society values such school skills. The philosophical foundations raise the question of whether that value is good or bad; perhaps, it can be argued, there are many other things the school can teach that are more important than what we think of as basic skills, such as concern for the welfare of others.

Other enduring problems explored in the philosophy of education raise similar questions concerning what is good or bad, which alternative is better or worse, *how* we should go about choosing among different policies of the school or among different teaching styles. So, the content of the philosophy of education may include a look at any one of hundreds of conflicting ideas about education and ways in which schools operate. Its major purpose is to help students discover how they themselves think about such conflicts, and how they can think more clearly about them as they later enter the profession.

Social. In the past this area drew primarily from sociology for its content, but recently the social foundations have included insights contributed by other social sciences, notably economics and anthropology. Some of the broad questions explored are: What is the connection between the school as a social institution and other institutions in society such as the family, the economic system, and the political order? What is the social impact of such policies as busing children to achieve school integration?

The social foundations' approach to perennial problems of education is very different from that of the other fields. It seeks to describe which groups in society press for different goals for education, and what effect these differences have on the schools. It asks—as new ethnic groups demand equal opportunity and more years of schooling—whether the school helps such groups achieve greater social and economic equality, or if that is just a myth. As different groups in society vie with one another to control what is taught, and how, it asks what the struggle shows about the power relations in society at large, and what effect that struggle has on the operation of the schools.

Some Problem Examples

One way to get the flavor of these different content areas as they take their unique stab at understanding education is to look briefly at a typical problem and the way it is handled.

One of the liveliest arguments going on in the foundations of education field, for example, is among the historians; it has to do with the question of how well the U.S. public school actually has succeeded in doing what it was supposed to do. About fifty years ago, historians of education believed that our public schools, during the nineteenth century, had done a superb job of helping the poor to overcome their problems and greatly improve their position in society. Our school system, these historians claimed, was a great engine of democracy, helping to equalize the condition of all American people. A different school of historians in the 1920s and 1930s, however, pointed out that the picture was not quite that rosy, that many immigrant children had failed in U.S. schools, and that many groups in the lower economic strata had been helped to achieve a better life by the churches and other community associations of their ethnic groups, rather than by the public schools. In the 1960s still another group of young historians began to argue that even that correction was wrong. What really happened, they wrote, is that U.S. public schools, whose administrators and teachers were white, middle-class, and Protestant, made things worse for immigrants and the other poor living in America's cities. Society was interested in keeping the poor quiet, and willing to work at mean, low-paying jobs, they argued, and used the school to make the children of these groups conform to society's expectation. Almost any course that students take in the historical foundations is likely to deal in one way or another with this controversy.

A major problem that inevitably comes to the surface in the philosophy of education is one that has been argued about since people began to discuss education. In fact, it is raised by the first of the great philosophers to consider education at all,

31

Plato. In his dialogue, the *Meno,* Plato raises the question: Can we train or educate people to be "good," that is, to achieve excellence as human beings? We can train them to play the flute, to write poetry, to be good soldiers, but can we educate them to develop what we nowadays call "good character?" Plato called it "virtue," and concluded that teachers can't make people virtuous, that only the gods can. If it *could* be done, he argued, surely men of virtue would raise their own children to be virtuous, and we have only to look about us to see how seldom that happens.

Yet, in the 2500 years since Plato wrote, there has seldom been a school that has not believed that it could teach boys and girls to be virtuous. Until fairly recently U.S. school teachers sent home report cards that, in addition to grades on reading, arithmetic, and social studies, rated children's leadership, perseverance, consideration for others, and similar character traits. So we apparently believe that we can imbue children with virtue. But even if we could do so, do we agree sufficiently on what makes "a virtuous person" to entrust the public schools with the task? Religious schools are another matter, but for the public schools the question turns out to be very difficult to answer.

Problems in the social foundations, in contrast to these, are more likely to involve the question of whether one state of things exists or does not, or which of several different explanations for a situation comes closest to being true. There is a considerable argument going on, for example, about who really has power over school policy in the 16,000 school districts across the country. Everyone agrees about who *should* have the most say in schools: the citizens and the parents. But they elect a district school board and delegate their authority to its members. That school board, in turn, hires a district school superintendent, and gives him or her authority to carry out the policies the board sets for its schools.

On the basis of their study of the current situation, some sociologists declare that the professional educators, the superintendents, are doing pretty much what they please, and that the school boards, which really represent the community, are simply doing what they are told. The superintendents themselves claim that their authority to run the schools has been

32

whittled down practically to zero, because aggressive special-interest groups in the community, just by making a lot of noise, can pressure the schools into doing what they want them to. Many of the topics in the social foundations are very much like this one; the student must look at the evidence that is used to support each conflicting claim, and try to determine which is more believable. In this instance, it is possible that both sides may be right; as other studies have shown, the question of power depends on the particular situation in a specific school district.

What Assignments Are Like

The educational foundations obviously are much like the ordinary academic courses all students are familiar with from both high school and the first year or two of college. Most of the assigned work consists of reading in either texts or special collections of journal articles. In historical foundations courses there is likely to be a basic textbook supplemented by smaller paperbacks covering special areas. As is the case with the discipline of history generally, reading assignments tend to be substantial.

Textbooks are used fairly frequently in the philosophical foundations courses, too, but there is a very good chance that students will instead be asked to read collections of original works from the long history of the development of educational ideas. Students may find some of these works a good deal more difficult to understand than a textbook, but they are usually more interesting and far more rewarding in many ways.

Such collections typically begin with Plato, usually the dialogue mentioned earlier and perhaps part of his greatest work, *The Republic,* and go on to a few works in the late middle ages, then to a number of writers in the eighteenth and nineteenth centuries whose ideas still directly influence modern schools. These include John Locke, Jean Jacques Rousseau, and Immanuel Kant. Larger sections of these collections include a wide variety of twentieth-century thinkers about education— often extensive selections from John Dewey, the most influential of U.S. educational philosophers.

Courses in social foundations show the widest variation in basic reading matter, depending on individual instructors' preferences. Textbooks for courses in the introduction to education are often very simply written, and filled with factual material on how schools are organized and what teachers do. Many instructors now use, instead of a textbook, a number of paperbacks chosen from among the flood of popular books on education published in the last decade. You will find some of them listed in the bibliography at the end of this book.

NOTES

[1] Henry C. Lindgren, *Educational Psychology in the Classroom*, 4th ed. (New York: John Wiley and Sons, 1972), p. 267.

3

Professional Course Work—
Elementary Sequence

The second major component in undergraduate teacher preparation, if you decide to teach at the elementary level, is a large block of credits devoted to an examination of the elementary-level curriculum and the study of the instructional skills necessary for teaching it. (The secondary sequence will be examined in the next chapter; either one or the other must be chosen.) It is an enormously diverse area of study as well as one for which the programs of teacher preparation institutions vary. With all the differences, however, there is a core of agreement on some requirements, and it is on these common elements that the following discussion will focus.

One such element, PBTE, is a fairly recent feature of the teacher preparation landscape. The initials stand for Performance-Based Teacher Education, although there is still another version of the program referred to as Competency-Based Teacher Education, or CBTE. The ideas that are part of this approach to teacher training surfaced in the 1960s and run something like this:

It is necessary that someone certify that beginning teachers are competent to teach, and the best agency to do so is the university that trains them. But it is not enough for that agency to assure its state department of education that graduates have taken and passed an appropriate number of courses, which is the way teachers were certified in the past. Schools of education and other responsible trainers should, in addition, be required to specify clearly the necessary knowledge and skills in which their graduates can demonstrate mastery. Thus, a grade of B in a course in Language Arts in the Elementary School may be sufficient proof for the registrar's office in the university that the student has the credit for the course toward a degree, but the state wants a specific assurance from the instructor of the course that, among other things, the student "can demonstrate the ability to develop reading-readiness among first-grade children."

Some elements of a performance-based program may now be found in all training institutions, though students will find some very different patterns available. A number of colleges, particularly in the midwest and on the west coast, have taken apart and rebuilt their entire teacher training curriculum on the basis of performance objectives. One Missouri college, for example, has defined hundreds of performance objectives, grouping related ones into a number of independent study units or "kits," and then asking students to work through them on their own, seeking faculty help only when necessary. Other institutions have retained traditional course work, and, indeed, the traditional courses, but they now state the course objectives in performance terms.

The examples of performance objectives given below are very typical of the kinds of statements students will confront as they enter teaching programs, though some lists of objectives may be much more specific than these. Each of them begins with "The teacher can . . ."

> . . . select curriculum materials in accordance with the developmental needs of students;
> . . . identify the prerequisites of a given learning objective;
> . . . model the types of behavior desired as student behavior;
> . . . use media, equipment, supplies, and technology appropriate to individual instructional situations;
> . . . organize class groups in such a manner that each student will know what is expected of him or her;
> . . . develop an atmosphere of shared decision making in the classroom;

... evaluate student performance on standards based on
objectives;

... demonstrate sensitivity to student rights, needs, feelings—including those of different ethnic, racial, and
religious groups;

... instill in students an appreciation of human diversity;

... preselect appropriate materials necessary to carry out
tasks.

Curriculum Course Content

The term "curriculum" is generally thought to mean whatever subjects are taught at a given level or in a particular
school. The more one looks at such an apparently simple field
of study, however, the more complicated it becomes. There has
never been very much agreement in this country about what to
teach in any area of knowledge, and, since most elementary
schools are supported with public funds, the disagreements can
and do become great public policy battles.

Curriculum also involves a great many educational problems
beyond questions of the subject matter to be taught, and to
which children. How should subject matter be arranged, in
separate bodies of knowledge or in relation to life problems?
Should children be exposed to the same learning tasks as a
group, or should they proceed through them at their individual pace? Are some subjects to be taught only by highly specialized personnel? On many such questions that relate to curriculum there are sharp differences of professional opinion,
and very often contradictory evidence about the effectiveness
of different answers.

Some training programs deal separately with the curriculum,
others include curriculum matters and related teaching skills in
the same course. In either case students are likely to be asked
to learn about the following content areas:

New Look at Old Themes

This means a replay of some of the subjects that may have
been touched on in a previous foundations course, but now

with a sharp focus on the elementary school: the historical development of the curriculum, philosophical conflicts over what should be taught in the early years, a review of learning theories applicable to the elementary grades, and a look at some of the social forces that now affect the work of the school at that level.

Curriculum Changes

These include the modern movement toward individualizing the curriculum to meet the interest of children. Some communities have found that the easiest way to meet that demand has been to provide "alternative schools" within the public school system, each with an emphasis on a particular curriculum. So, one elementary school might be especially rich in opportunities to develop musical talent and interest, another might emphasize mathematics, and so forth. These new approaches may very well break down the traditional neighborhood-school idea in the long run.

The desire to individualize, and therefore to move toward specialization, has led to a number of other innovations. The "non-graded primary" organizes the early grades of the elementary school into individual progress units: instead of moving from first grade to second grade together, for example, individual children move at their own pace through a number of levels of achievement in reading and arithmetic, taking progress tests on their own when ready.

Learning Materials

Most attention devoted to texts and other aids to learning is part of later considerations of specific areas of the curriculum: mathematics, reading, science, etc. Somewhere in the professional course work, however, there is usually coverage, on a general level, of educational resources: when it is most appropriate to use them, and how they compare with one another in effectiveness. Students are likely to be asked to review textbooks in a number of curriculum areas, to learn how programmed texts work and how children respond to them, as well as how to introduce children to auto-instructional machines, including language laboratory equipment. They will also learn about the enormous resources available on records, film, and slide film and what to use them for, about television resources, and the many uses of the community as a learning laboratory.

Curriculum Theory

In the skill areas such as reading and arithmetic, recent efforts by university subject-area experts to improve what public elementary and secondary schools teach have concentrated on ways of motivating children, and on the development of an extraordinary array of well-worked-out materials. Both of these are linked to several interesting new curriculum theories in science, social studies, and literature.

A good example of a new approach is the "spiral curriculum," developed in the social studies. Educators realized that many of the facts and concepts taught in such subjects as geography and history became rapidly out of date in the modern world, and that children were being required to remember many facts for which they had no organizing scheme. In a search for a longer lasting and more basic kind of knowledge, educators have worked out a way of teaching what is called the "structure" of the social sciences—the basic concepts that are used to explain human behavior and society. The same concepts can be taught through the elementary grades at higher levels of abstractness as the child gets older, and in relation to different areas of social life.

The term "spiral" is applied to such a curriculum because the child returns to the same concepts at a higher level each time, as can be seen in the example in Figure 1. The concepts are: *cultural change, interdependence,* and *cooperation,* applied in the first grade to the family, the simplest social group and the closest to the child's experience, and by the sixth grade to nations, the most complicated and abstract group. Much the same approach has been worked out for science and mathematics.

Curriculum Areas

Language Arts. The most basic and serious business of the elementary grades is to teach children to read and write at

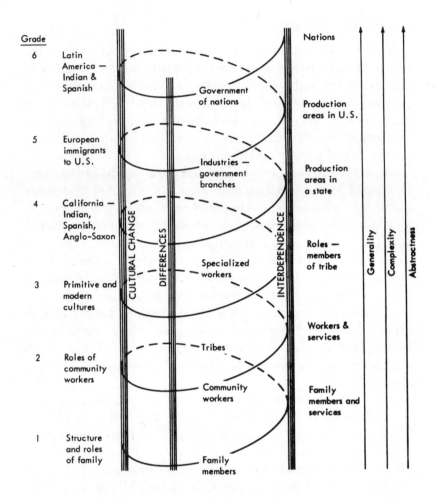

Figure 1. The Spiral of Concept Development

Source: Taba, *Teachers' Handbook for Elementary Social Studies* (c) 1967, Addison-Wesley, Reading, Mass., p. 15. Reprinted with permission.

40

some acceptable level of competence. There is nothing the schools do that is more argued about, nothing that draws so much public criticism and debate as the area of language arts.

Although students will find that the greatest emphasis in teacher-training programs is on the *methods* of teaching reading, the curriculum aspects of the reading program are important because they provide a needed overall view of the process of learning to read. Curriculum texts, for example, are likely to treat reading skill as only one of many communication skills that must be taught in the elementary schools, one of the most important of which is *listening*. Because people must take in a good deal of the information they need through listening, a number of experts believe that the skills involved should be taught throughout the school years and that a good beginning must be made before reading instruction begins.

Students will be introduced to a number of general approaches to the reading curriculum so that, in a field that features a good deal of conflict over what is most effective, they can later make their own choices in developing a teaching style. There has been much argument, for example, over the question of how best to teach children in the earliest stage of "breaking the code" of the written word. Should we start them off by having them get used to recognizing whole words (like "hat" and "rat"), or by learning the sounds of the letters and how to put them together to form words? Most of that argument has now been settled, in what is called the "eclectic" approach— in which both methods are used.

More recently, curriculum experts have been concerned about the rival claims of two other approaches. One of these emphasizes using children's experiences for writing stories and reports that then become the materials for their reading practice. Some experts favor, instead, the use of *basal readers*, which present carefully developed sequences of words and phrases, with a good deal of repetition to ensure learning. The language-experience approach relates better to children's life experience and environment, but many experts feel that very important concepts do not appear often enough or systematically enough for effective learning: a child growing up in a small town, for instance, may never encounter zoos, apartment buildings, or the subway.

As children master the very basic skills of reading and listening (by the third grade), the curriculum becomes much more varied. The whole world of children's literature opens up, and the school can begin to teach critical reading and the use of the written word to enrich one's life. Both descriptive and creative writing enter the curriculum as increasingly important objectives, and by the sixth grade, teaching and learning activities begin to resemble the familiar communications courses of high school and college, though on a vastly simpler level.

Mathematics and Science. Few areas of the elementary school curriculum have undergone as much change in recent years as math and science. One result has been to diversify the way in which teacher training programs have tended to handle these subjects; students are much more likely now to take courses in them as separate fields, rather than, as before, combined in a single course.

Mathematics instruction in particular has taken new forms, so much so that parents these days are apt to throw up their hands in frustration when their children ask for help with math homework. Instead of the old emphasis on routine and memorization, the new math can be recognized by the following trends. First, "number" is taught as a concept, and so are other mathematical properties and operations that, if they were taught at all, were previously given to pupils as operations to be learned without fully being understood. Second, not only is understanding of concepts stressed, but a great deal of effort is devoted to helping pupils "discover" the concepts themselves, at least in a primitive form. The approach is referred to as the discovery method, and most modern materials produced for the elementary grades use it at least part of the time. Third, mathematical concepts that used to be taught first in high school or even in college are now being brought down in a simplified form (the spiral curriculum again) for pupils in the early grades. Ideas about probability, sets, functions and functional relations, and logical thinking, among others, are now taught quite early.

A similar revolution in science education has produced a shift from the learning of simple theory and fact to a pronounced emphasis on the *processes* of science. Here the discovery approach is very frequently used to involve pupils in laboratory-like experiments with materials, from which they are encouraged to develop their own explanations. Science experts have been especially ingenious in developing simple, but powerful, experiments for pupils to perform with inexpensive materials like matchsticks, rubber bands, and waterglasses.

The shape of the science curriculum, as evidenced by the subjects covered in the early grades, has also drastically changed. The enormous popular interest in the environment and its science, ecology, is mirrored in the curriculum emphasis on the earth sciences generally. What was once a few rather dull units on physical health has expanded into a much broader consideration of both physical and mental well-being. In many school systems, it has branched into a serious look at sex and its implications for children, and become a carefully planned six- to twelve-year "family life" program. As an example of the new freedom in such subjects, here are the specific objectives at the K-3 level for a "family life" in a midwestern city:

> To build a wholesome attitude toward sex.
> To know and understand the sex differences in boys and girls.
> To know and use the correct terminology in reference to the body.
> To understand the nature and purpose of the family, and the obligation to be a good family member, with loyalty, love, and respect.
> To understand and respect all parts of the body, which includes the organs of elimination.
> To lessen and prevent unnecessary handling of the body.
> To discuss with openness and lack of embarrassment the problem of growing up sexually.
> To know the elementary facts of reproduction.

Social Studies. The revolution in the social studies curriculum proceeded a little later, perhaps, than the reforms described in math and science. Complaints about the social studies in the elementary school were much the same: too much memorization of facts, not enough attention to processes such as problem solving, allowing history, geography, and civics to retain their traditional hold on the curriculum instead of encouraging other, and newer, areas of study such as sociology, anthropology, and political science.

However, social scientists from these and other subject areas could not agree as easily about what should be taught as those in the physical sciences, math and language arts. New social-studies programs sprouted in school systems across the country, funded mainly by the federal government, and took a great variety of new approaches. Teacher training courses explore, for example, such common elements among these approaches as:

1. A much greater emphasis on the social sciences instead of a pure diet of history and government. This includes, in some programs, rare disciplines (rare to the elementary years, at any rate) such as law, social psychology, and economics.

2. A spiral-curriculum approach to the study of important concepts, such as civil rights and community.

3. As in the natural sciences, an attempt to lead children, through discovery learning, to develop their own explanations for the problems and conflicts of modern social life. The materials provided for that search for meaning are vastly more interesting and varied than ever before in the social studies, requiring a good deal more flexibility on the part of the teacher.

4. More attention to teaching some of the skills of the social sciences: gathering evidence and interpreting it, critical thinking, and the analysis of social values.

5. In many programs an emphasis on non-Western peoples and their societies, at least partly to encourage, over the long run, international understanding. Along much the same track there is also a new focus on the experience of Third-World peoples (such as Africans, Asians, Hispanics, and Amerindians) in their lives as minorities within the countries of the West.

The Arts. A last major area that will invariably be considered in professional course work, and much more seriously than it often was in the past, includes the visual and plastic arts, the performing arts, and music. Not only have these areas of both appreciation and skills taken a more noticeable place in the elementary curriculum as separate objectives for learning, but they are much better integrated than before into the major content areas. Works of art are studied as part of social life in units on sociology and anthropology, and as ways of gaining a deeper understanding of past societies in the study of history.

Students are likely to find a considerable confusion, however, on the question of how the arts are to be integrated into the program as a whole. Should the regular classroom teacher also take responsibility for the arts curriculum, or should specialized teachers with more expert knowledge and skills in the arts take over? One alternative to these two possibilities, *team teaching,* is certain to be discussed. A team of teachers, one member an art specialist, can cooperatively plan demonstrations and lessons that combine the expertise of the specialist with the intimate knowledge of the children possessed by the classroom teacher. A good proportion of the professional course work makes students familiar with just this kind of solution for curriculum problems: a solution that attempts to bring into harmony subject matter expertise, new ideas about school organization innovations, and teaching methodology.

Along with some specialized work in the arts, most colleges also require their students to have some familiarity with physical education in the elementary school, the activities and games that are appropriate for that age level, and how the field fits into the general curriculum of the early childhood years.

Elementary School Teaching Methods

Teacher training programs offer a wide variety of experiences generally considered to be part of the "methods" area in a series of at least two courses. A good deal of this work is now being done in the schools themselves, rather than in the college classroom, in various forms of clinical programs that will be described in a later chapter. However, some basic knowledge of teaching methods and skills can be taught more efficiently in a regular college classroom, either before or during the time that students are working in the real world of the school.

The diagram below presents some of the major types of objectives related to teaching methods; as one moves down the funnel shape toward more and more specific things to be learned by children, the narrower and more practical are the

45

skills to be learned by the teacher. The rest of this chapter describes some typical training objectives at each level, the kinds of assignments students are often required to complete, and what goes on in class.

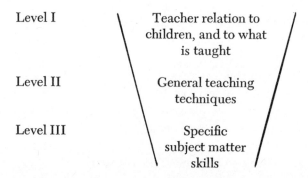

Level I — Teacher relation to children, and to what is taught

Level II — General teaching techniques

Level III — Specific subject matter skills

Level I: Some Contrasting Teaching Approaches

Much of the talk, and some argument, about basic teaching emphases these days centers around "humanistic" teaching versus "behavior modification." Although these conceptual terms are used here to illustrate some of the approaches that students will be exposed to, you should be warned that the differences between them are often somewhat exaggerated; it may be perfectly possible to develop a teaching style that draws on both.

The humanist teacher. Although humanist educators grant that teachers must be well prepared in the subject matter they must teach, they regard teaching primarily as a human relationship. So, for example, teachers must have a very accurate understanding of people and their behavior, because they will act, as teachers, on the basis of their beliefs about people. Humanists would argue that teachers who believe that their children can learn and who have confidence in their ability, will be more successful than teachers who do not have confidence in the ability of their children, particularly with those pupils who already have a history of failure.

For humanists, these beliefs about the self are the most important aspect of teaching; teachers who believe that all children can and will learn, encourage pupils to develop a positive self-concept, one that includes self-confidence about learning.

This is one of the basic ways in which teachers *use themselves as instruments*: they use their own beliefs, feelings, and thoughts, as tools to change the beliefs and feelings of pupils, and thus, their behavior and achievements.

There is no "humanist teaching method," therefore. Teacher education programs must help each student find the method that suits his or her purposes best, because teaching is a unique expression of an individual's personality. But, although one cannot, therefore, teach common methods, humanists do try to get students to share common purposes, purposes that they believe result in the most effective learning for children. Such purposes include:

> freeing, rather than controlling, pupils
> involving children with large, rather than small, problems and issues
> revealing oneself, rather than concealing oneself, *being* oneself at all times
> becoming personally involved with others, instead of being aloof
> helping processes along, rather than "achieving goals"

Putting the education student into personal contact with the human situation of teaching is clearly an absolute necessity for the humanist instructor. Training programs that emphasize this approach to teaching do, indeed, pay a great deal of attention to human interaction; assigned readings are likely to be mostly books and articles written by teachers who are trying to communicate the meaning of their own experiences with children. Out-of-class assignments are likely to require thinking about and describing on paper (or outlining for an oral presentation) some experience in a school in which students spent some of their time, or a discussion among a small group of classmates.

Classes themselves, in this type of program, might well be small in size; might be informal, with chairs in a circle, or around a table, first names, etc.; consist almost entirely of discussion rather than lecture; have decisions on activities made by students and teacher together; and devote a sizeable proportion of time to planning what students will read, what they will discuss, etc.

A notable feature of this approach is the use of small group exercises that put students into situations in which they can explore the meanings of personal relationships with other students. For example, a common practice in the human-relations laboratories that are often included in teacher-training programs is to divide a classroom group into pairs of students. The partners meet on their own two or three times during the semester and work together through a series of exercises for which instructions are provided. They might, typically, spend some of their time together revealing and clarifying personal goals and how they relate to the goals of the course, following a guide like this one:

1. Decide who will be the first to be interviewed.
2. Conduct a ten-minute interview, focusing on the questions below. The interviewer should feed back to the Interviewee a paraphrase after each answer. The goals are openness and accurate listening. Do *not* take notes.
3. After ten minutes switch roles and repeat the process.
4. Take three minutes to talk with your partner about the interviewing experience.
5. Give a brief report to the total group on the person you interviewed.

Interview questions in such exercises include:

1. What personal goals do you have toward which you might work in this class?
2. What concerns do you have about this class so far? (Be as specific as possible.)
3. What concerns are you willing to share with the class (for example, concerns about particular class members, how you see yourself, your impact on the class, your interpersonal relationships)?

Evaluation of student performance or achievement in a humanist program is likely to be informal. Although grades must be given because the college itself requires them, they may be assigned simply for completion of specific activities; for example, two written observations of children in school get a B, four observations get an A. Some humanist instructors believe that the process of grading is so destructive that they simply tell students in advance that all will receive A's at the end of the semester.

Behaviorism. This contrasting approach to the process of teaching developed out of a way of looking at learning based on a psychology that concentrates on peoples' behavior rather than what they believe, or how they feel. Students are not likely to find a whole teacher-training program based on it, as is the case with the humanist approach, but individual instructors may well emphasize it.

Behaviorism has an *engineering* feel to it. Teaching, it suggests, is largely a matter of managing the rational process of having learners acquire new behavior. Complicated skills, such as reading, can be broken down into a number of simpler skills that learners can master in a proper sequence. The key to mastery lies not in whether children believe they can learn, or how they feel about themselves, but in rewarding them properly. "Reward" can consist of grades, approval, or just being told that one has done the correct thing.

The most basic principles in this approach is: behavior that is reinforced (rewarded) will tend to occur again, and again, until it is firmly in the control of the learner. Anyone who has learned to swim or to dance under someone's expert instruction can illustrate the principle: the not-very-successful first tries, receiving criticism of the wrong moves and approval for the right ones (reward), practice of smaller units of the entire process until they become smooth, and the achievement of final mastery of the entire skill.

The teaching methods course of the behaviorist will not have the informal, free setting of the humanist's course. Instructors are more likely to have in mind very specific, clearly stated teaching skills that they want students to learn and practice. The course may well be based on a very detailed workbook with practical teaching skill exercises for students to work on outside of class. Class time itself may be tightly organized into half-hour or forty-five-minute modules devoted to concrete, limited skills; students practice teaching a very brief lesson, then try it again after suggestions and criticisms are made. Some universities have elaborate set-ups for videotaping these "microteaching" experiences so that students can study their own performance along with the rest of the class.

49

Level II: General Teaching Techniques

Before these courses get down to the nuts and bolts of teaching, they deal with an intermediate level that concerns the techniques used in a variety of teaching settings. Two contrasting illustrations of methods at this level are provided below .

Lesson Planning. Developing a lesson plan is surely the most traditional and routine of all the things teachers are trained to do. Instructors who are thoroughly committed to a humanist approach are likely to skip it altogether. Some teachers who get stuck with a principal who mindlessly demands a lesson plan for every hour of the day, whether teachers follow it or not, claim that they suffer the torments of the damned.

But, learning to plan a lesson can be very helpful, if the plan includes a sensible amount of detail, and if the teacher is willing to depart from the plan to seize some momentary opportunity of an unusual class happening. Not only can it be a lifeline for the beginning teacher, just as detailed notes may be for an after-dinner speaker, but it can also serve the more experienced teacher who wants to try out a new idea or add a learning objective not attempted before. In the course of writing a lesson plan, teachers must work through such problems as:

> defining for themselves very clearly what the children are supposed to learn in the lesson (and thus providing themselves with a clearer idea too)

> deciding on the way in which a diagnosis will be made of what the children do and do not know in the area to be covered by the lesson (and *which* children know what)

> selecting the best possible instructional materials for the learning objectives (and getting them duplicated in time to have them on hand when needed)

> determining which skills involved in the lesson's objectives require some practice, and deciding whether individual or group practice is best

> finding places in the lesson where it would be useful to ask for pupil ideas, and deciding how to make use of these contributions

> setting aside time, either just after the lesson or sometime

later, to evaluate how well children have learned what the lesson was intended to teach, and to decide how to measure this

Interaction Analysis.   A very different example of an intermediate skill, to which some teacher training programs give a great deal of attention, involves the use of the Verbal Interaction Category System (VICS), designed to help teachers become aware of the importance of verbal behavior in the classroom, and to use it to improve the learning situation.

Talk between teachers and pupils, and among pupils themselves, makes up a large proportion of what goes on in the classroom, as many studies have shown. VICS was originated to enable teachers to develop the kind of verbal patterns within the classroom that are most likely to get the learning results they desire, instead of simply repeating the teaching styles of their own past teachers.

VICS consists of a set of categories for identifying any single bit of interaction in the classroom. Students can themselves apply the system by analyzing videotapes of their own attempts to teach a lesson; or an observer (often another student) can do the analysis and provide the results to a fellow student engaged in practicing a particular teaching skill. The major categories of the system are listed below, to provide some idea of what the activity is like:

1. Teacher-initiated talk:
    —Gives information or opinion, presents content, explains, etc.
    —Gives directions, orders, commands, etc.
    —Asks narrow questions, as in drill, requiring yes-no answers, etc.
    —Asks broad questions, open-ended, thought-provoking, etc.
2. Teacher response:
    —*Accepts* ideas, behavior, or feelings of pupils
    —*Rejects* ideas, behavior, or feelings of pupils
3. Pupil response:
    —Responds to teacher in short, predictable replies
    —Responds to teacher in broad, unpredictable replies
    —Responds to another pupil

4. Pupil initiates talk:
   —directly to teacher, not as response
   —directly to another pupil, not as a response
5. Other talk:
   —pauses or short periods of silence
   —confusion

Level III: Specific Teaching Methods

Finally, at the most concrete level, methods courses deal practically and in detail with preparing students to make the kinds of daily decisions they will later have to make on their own in the classroom: decisions about classroom management, about taking pupils through appropriate learning steps, and so on.

There is a vast array of practical advice about methods and concrete procedures to follow. In recent years there has been a movement away from detailed descriptions of methods and in favor of workbooks and exercises that guide the teaching students' own thinking about planning and development of specific lessons. The location of much of this instruction has also moved into the school itself, in field situations that will be described in a later chapter. A few illustrations of more academic activities are given here to convey the flavor of the students' work at this level.

Breaking a learning goal into specific objectives. The first section of this chapter described the way in which teacher education, in many colleges, has been based on specific statements of teacher competencies emphasized in a given program. Exactly the same approach has been taken to define the learning behavior of pupils. A methodology commonly taught to teachers-to-be, therefore, includes reducing a general learning objective to a number of very specific parts. Such a breakdown of general goals includes:

defining two parts of the goal: (1), the subject matter content (2), what the pupil must do with the content
making the subject-matter part as specific as possible; for example, listing the items of knowledge composing it

specifically defining the student's behavior in relation to the content; for example, "the student demonstrates the ability to apply the concept in an unfamiliar example"

identifying the level of performance that will determine achievement of the goal; for example, "the student will accurately identify 8 out of 10 important dates of the American Revolution that are presented"

In a typical assignment to be worked on independently and discussed later in class, students might be required to select a subject matter that interests them and a grade level at which they intend to teach (e.g., a fifth grade science unit on the water cycle), and list the general goals. Then, for each of the goals, they must write specific objectives that satisfy the standards above. For example: "Presented with a diagram of the water cycle, students should be able to label correctly seven of eight important parts of the process"; or "Presented with a problem in the water supply of a large city, students should be able to suggest a possible problem in the water cycle that would explain why the difficulty has occurred."

A learning activity dealing with concepts. Here's an example of an even more concrete teaching method, as it might be presented in an assignment for college students.

As the curriculum of the elementary school has shifted from a heavy emphasis on rote learning to the study of broader concepts, teachers have had to learn how to introduce children to the meaning of "concept" itself. In the most basic sense, a concept is an abstract category that defines a set of standards for including real things in the category. "Mammal" is a concept that separates one category of "animals" from other categories of animals. Here is a learning activity from a teaching methods workbook that provides practice in a method that might later be used with children in a classroom.[1]

> For this activity, you will need a group of five to eight persons and a collection of three or more old magazines with pictures in them. These should be magazines you are willing to part with, for they will be destroyed in the activity. The exercise demonstrates in an entertaining way how we employ conceptual categories to organize and sort out information. Follow these steps once your group is organized.

53

1. Set a time limit of ten minutes, and begin to tear out of the magazines all the pictures that interest you.
2. Arbitrarily halt the picture-collecting process at the end of the time limit.
3. Sort the collection of pictures into three piles.
4. Think of a one-word or two-word label for each of the piles.
5. Share your choices in the piles and the labels. Then indicate the rationale for the labels.
6. Discuss the similarities and differences in the choices.

NOTES

[1] James M. Cooper *et al.*, *Classroom Teaching Skills, A Workbook* (Lexington, Mass.: D. C. Heath, 1977), p. 148.

4

Professional Course Work— Secondary Sequence

The part of the education sequence devoted to curriculum and methods for students intending to teach in the secondary school is much more compressed than for the elementary level. Most secondary students' time is, of course, spent in studying the specialty they intend to teach, and in some colleges students must major in their specialty. Attention to professional issues, such as curriculum and methods, is commonly compressed into a few courses, though some teaching methods are occasionally discussed in the major courses themselves.

Secondary School Organization

The vast majority of secondary sequences devotes at least part of the allotted professional course work to a look at the ways in which secondary education is organized in this country. The simple school structure of the previous century— eight years of elementary and four years of high school—has in our time turned into a great variety of patterns. Trying to gain an understanding of why this has happened, and the meaning of the continuing search for a way to educationally structure the adolescent years, is a useful and interesting exploration for future teachers.

Middle School

The appropriate dividing line between a child and a youth, for instance, is a question that educators seem unable to resolve for very long, although they all seem to agree that some special form of school is needed to separate the pre-adolescent from the adolescent period. The junior high school, covering grades seven, eight, and nine, which fulfilled that role for a period of thirty or forty years, no longer has very many strong defenders. Ideas about what should take its place are not in short supply, and the argument about which idea is the best forms the subject matter of courses that deal with what is now called the "middle school." Topics students are likely to encounter in such a course include:

> A description of the recent move, in school systems across the country, toward new middle-school patterns, who is behind it, and how widespread the movement has become.
>
> The criticisms of the traditional 6-3-3 pattern, with the junior high school in the middle, and why some educators think it does not fit what we now know about the growth and development of young people.
>
> Surveys of various patterns that school districts are trying out, for example, grades 5-8, 6-8, 6-9, etc.
>
> Descriptions of the ways in which the curriculum is organized in the different systems, and how organization of the pupils' time forms a bridge between the close supervision of younger pupils in the elementary school to the greater freedom of the high school youngster.
>
> Detailed descriptions of some of the most interesting of the new middle schools and some assessment of how well they are succeeding.
>
> Considerations of teaching methods that may be most appropriate for pupils in these middle years.

Students particularly interested in the possibilities of teaching in these new kinds of school may find it useful to shop about for an educational sequence that specializes in preparing teachers for this level. Instead of superficially covering such topics as those listed above in part of one professional course, an entire year-long study focused exclusively on the middle school will probably include the following elements: a course in the dynamics of the behavior of the pre-adolescent; intensive work on the background necessary to create tests suitable for use with a middle-school population of pupils; a curriculum course that examines the total development of the course of study from kindergarten through high school, so that future middle school teachers can see where their own slices of subject matter fit; and, finally, practice teaching in a middle school.

Such specialized programs are more likely to be found at the graduate level, to prepare those who are already teaching in either an elementary or a high school for a shift to the new form of school. They will increasingly be offered at the undergraduate level, however, as the movement grows. A student decision to head in the direction of teaching in the middle school can well be made at the undergraduate level, in any event, and should involve thinking through some of the following questions early in the undergraduate career:

1. *Am I interested in developing scholarship in a special academic field, and do I have the ability to do so?* A "yes" answer to this question does not necessarily demonstrate the kind of commitment to a subject field that high school teachers should have, but must go beyond the interest of the average elementary teacher in a special area of knowledge.

2. *Would I like working with pre-adolescents and older children?* It helps to have had some experience as a camp counselor, or in a similar job, in finding an honest answer to this one. Young people at this stage are deeply engaged in a search for self, and their relations to adults around them are a great strain on some of those adults. Their greatest need, perhaps, is for stable and secure adults who will not feel rebuffed, for example, if these children reject attempts to help them.

3. *Do I like working with others as a team, or do I prefer working on my own?* Teachers in the elementary school, for the most part, spend their time in "the self-contained classroom," with a great deal of control over their own activities with a single group of children.

High school teachers meet with several different groups during the day, but again on their own. Most of the new forms of middle schools emphasize team teaching, in which a group of teachers must plan and carry out a series of activities as part of a shared operation.

4. *Do I like an atmosphere in which activities undergo frequent change, and in which there is a constant search for new ways of doing things?* The middle-school movement is itself in search of workable innovations, and teachers in these schools have to be prepared for a good deal of experiment and for having people look over their shoulders much of the time to find out how things are working out. Those who prefer a stable situation would be advised to take their training at some other level.

High School

The problem of the middle school, as treated in courses within the secondary education sequence, is one example of the units of instruction that look at the total question of organizing the years of schooling. A much greater emphasis, in the typical secondary program, is given to the dominant form of secondary schooling, the high school.

Both the curriculum and the organization of the U.S. high school have gone through a number of revolutionary changes in the hundred years or so since the high school stopped being a small college-preparation agency for a highly select group of youngsters. Students preparing to teach at the secondary level will be exposed to such fairly recent innovations as:

Splitting large schools into smaller units (either within the same building or nearby) in which pupils can get to know their fellow students and the faculty better

Non-graded high schools that emphasize individual progress based on independent study

Flexible time scheduling, permitting the school to fit its program to individual needs instead of requiring the student to fit into the rigid schedule of the school

Changes in staffing patterns, including such devices as team teaching

All these new procedures, in concert with curriculum changes that have loosened up traditional requirements, are part of what can be viewed as a humanistic movement at the secondary level of schooling designed to make schools more flexible and adaptive to the various needs of students.

Flexible scheduling, for example, is an innovation that was developed as high school educators began to see the need to depart from a rigid schedule of forty-five- or fifty-minute periods throughout the day. Some courses, they reasoned, need more time than others; some classes may need to meet fewer times, but for longer periods.

One response to these needs was to develop a schedule composed of much shorter periods (twenty or thirty minutes, perhaps), so that one course could meet briefly every day, another could schedule three periods together on two days, and so on.

Even greater flexibility can be achieved by incorporating team teaching into a schedule. For example, a team of six teachers may be given responsibility for 181 students for a two-hour block of time each day. The group may be split up in any way the team finds useful, for time periods that fit the activity. The entire group might watch a half-hour film or a laboratory demonstration, then break into several thirty-pupil groups for a follow-up lecture, and a number of smaller discussion groups under the supervision of another member of the teaching team, with the remaining students dispersed in the library or in resource rooms working on their own.

Many texts point out that the difficulty posed by some of these organizational changes in the high school is that teachers fall so in love with a particular flexible schedule that they proceed to "freeze it" into a routine as rigid as the traditional schedule. Problems such as these usually form the content of class discussion and outside assignments for the college student. Here, for example, are some of the questions for discussion on this issue of scheduling, posed by one of the nationally used texts in secondary education:[1]

1. Hold a brainstorming discussion on "the ideal secondary school schedule." What do you and your col-

leagues recommend in order to return the control over time to teachers and pupils?

2. Prepare a statement defending or objecting to a current regulation of your state education department or regional accrediting agency which specifies a given number of minutes per week for a selected course or subject.

3. As a teacher, what would you do if you had more time free from scheduled contacts with groups of pupils?

Curriculum Problems

There are a number of curriculum problems that are particularly identified with the high school years. At some point in their professional courses students in secondary sequences will find themselves exploring at least some of the following issues:

1. Should all high school students be expected to graduate and receive diplomas? If so, is there some body of knowledge and skills that we should insist that they master before they receive the diploma? There are few topics in education that are as sharply debated as this one, because it raises sensitive questions about why some groups of young people do much less well in high school than other groups. Because everyone is supposed not only to go to high school but to graduate, schools and teachers have been under great pressure to pass all students along, without regard to how much they have learned. As a result, in recent years, the public has discovered that pupils who are almost illiterate are receiving high school diplomas. Education students are usually encouraged to develop their own opinions on complex issues of this kind.

2. How shall high school pupils be grouped for instruction? This is a problem that has been around for a long time, and has not become any easier with the years. As high school entry was expanded and all youth encouraged to attend, not only did differences in ability show up more sharply, but differences in interest also appeared. When the high school was an elite school, serving only a small fraction of youth, most high school students intended to go on to college, and did so. The percent-

age of college-bound students has vastly increased since the year 1900, but half of all high school graduates today do not go to college, and many who do, attend two-year colleges or technical institutes for which traditional high school courses do not seem to be necessary. But, having college-bound students attend separate high schools (the original answer to the problem) seems undemocratic to many people. One current answer is to have students attend comprehensive high schools, whatever future they have in mind, and to group them in separate "tracks" within the school. This kind of separation now seems just as undemocratic to some, and is the subject of much debate in college course work as well as among the public.

3. Shall we organize curriculum content into separate courses by subject matter (biology, English literature, history, etc.) or by life experience and needs? This is a question that, as the preceding chapter pointed out, is also a lively issue at the elementary school level. But the problem is a more difficult one for the high school, because, as those who support organizing by traditional subjects argue, high schools must prepare pupils for a college curriculum that does stress separate fields of study. This is not only true of liberal-arts work in college, but of such vocational and professional areas as engineering, which require evidence of work in mathematics, science, and the like. Some curriculum experts prefer a curriculum in which separate subject fields are brought to bear on important life needs. Instruction in "family living," for example, should draw on home economics, mathematics, social studies, fine arts, biology, and so on. Or, understanding the concept of "democracy" also requires study of a number of different areas of knowledge.

Such basic issues as these may precede or follow the major curriculum focus of the introductory course in the secondary professional sequence: a review of all of the important subjects that the high school teaches. Even though students are preparing to teach in only one, or at the most, two, fields, most teacher preparation programs consider it important that they see their own special subject as it fits into the total curriculum. That is surely the way in which high school students themselves will see it.

The curriculum review typically includes chapters or sections covering the following areas:

Business and sales programs
English language arts
Fine arts and performing arts
Foreign languages
Home economics
Industrial arts
Mathematics
Physical education and health
Science
Social Studies
Vocational education

The last category on the list, vocational education, is itself composed of a number of separate fields, each of them offering distinct career opportunities. Some of these fields are supported by substantial investment of federal funds; home economics is one of these and is described below, and so is agriculture, a popular curriculum specialty in rural-area high schools. The federal Vocational Education Act of 1963 now offers funds for other vocational fields, such as business education, as well. Schools of education often specialize in one or another of these fields, and strong programs in a wide variety of them are generally found only in the larger state university systems.

Instead of selecting a traditional academic subject as an example of how a typical secondary curriculum course might deal with one of these curriculum areas, we have chosen a specialized subject, home economics. Students are usually asked to consider some of the following issues in that field:

How home economics developed as a curriculum area. It was once called "domestic science," for instance, and forced down the throats of all girls who weren't determined to do something with their lives other than become wives and homemakers. But, for half a century, there has been a sizeable amount of federal money to support, improve, and innovate education in this area, and, as a consequence, federal agencies have required a great deal more than the cooking and sewing that used to dominate home economics. In many high schools the program will, as a result, include child care, family relationships, money management, becoming a critical consumer, and many other issues. The chemistry and physiology of nutrition may be taught, in addition to the pertinent role of economics.

Should boys enroll? Changing ideas about sex roles have led many schools to assign boys and girls at random to such courses as home economics and woodworking. Others develop special home economics courses for boys and urge them to attend. This is still a curriculum issue that is very much open to debate, though it is clear that some parts of the field may provide excellent preparation for later vocations—for example, hotel and restaurant management.

What is happening to the American family? Observers of the high school curriculum must confront the question of whether anything like "domestic science" makes sense in a country in which over half of the married women have jobs outside the family and in which parents live many years past the time that their children have grown and left home. Some educators insist that it is just *because* of these new strains on family life that high school youth must learn more about the family and how to make it better. It is clear, at any rate, that the aims of home economics courses must be changed as the nature of the family changes.

These and similar questions form the subject of class discussion and out-of-class study. The questions themselves suggest a number of ways in which curriculum problems in one area of study may become closely linked to problems in other areas. Notice, for example, how the three home economics issues described relate to questions that might usefully be dealt with in high school courses in health education, or social studies.

Classroom Management

A very important area within the professional course sequence deals with a set of problems that usually head the list of anxieties shared by most teachers-to-be. It is sometimes referred to as "maintaining order in the classroom," or "discipline." The heading for this section is the more neutral term that teacher trainers tend to use.

63

It is not just a problem for beginners—60 percent of all teachers in a national survey recognize it as their "most important" or an "important" problem. Gallup polls dealing with education usually find that the public puts "problems of discipline" at or near the top of the list of concerns about the schools. The most common teacher complaint about college education courses is that they did not provide enough preparation for handling groups of adolescents who are not only "all over the place," but often in a stage of growth in which resisting authority seems like a fine idea.

Professional courses try to help the future teacher in several ways. One of these is to provide background in adolescent psychology leading to an understanding of common behavior patterns of youth during that period, in the hope that teachers armed with that understanding will not react blindly to certain types of behavior. This kind of material may well have been covered in earlier foundations courses in psychology, but it is likely to have different meaning for students at this point in the education sequence.

Here is a textbook illustration of this approach. While some of the blame for discipline problems is put on the problem student, the teacher is expected to react professionally instead of impulsively:[2]

> Teachers, like other human beings, will react negatively to anyone who makes life more difficult for them. It would require a kind of superman to react with loving kindness toward a sixteen-year-old who continually makes irritating remarks in class. They might easily develop a healthy dislike for such a youngster. Under ordinary circumstances, that is, if he were not a teacher, his attitude might not matter so much. But the teaching situation is not an ordinary circumstance, and the teacher is not justified in reacting as he would in a normal social situation. Dislike is a strong impediment to providing help. Yet the students who need help most are almost always those who are most difficult to like.

A second approach that usually accompanies this one is to suggest to the students the possible cause for discipline problems that may not primarily have to do with high school youngsters themselves, but rather with the teacher or the situation.

Secondary texts discuss, for example, the following school situations that commonly lead to classroom disorder:

Last period of the day
Just before lunch
The day preceding an important school sport event
The period immediately following a break in the school routine, such as a fire drill
Fridays, generally
A substitute teacher

Other discipline problems are discussed as difficulties arising mostly from behavior of the teachers, such as:

Sarcasm and impoliteness
Having favorites
Failing to make assignments and directives clear
Never varying a constant routine
Failing to take account of individual differences

Students will encounter the problems of classroom management again in later methods courses, and later still in student teaching. All along this route the kind of analysis illustrated above is usually supplemented by discussions of cases and by role-playing typical discipline problems.

Secondary School Teaching Methods

There is a great deal of variety in teaching methods at this level, due simply to differences in subject matter. The foreign-language teacher must learn some very special methods that the social studies teacher need not. But students in the secondary sequence will find some common elements, too, in what they must learn about teaching.

High school teachers, like elementary grade teachers, must learn to make lesson plans and to clarify for themselves the learning aims they have in mind for their pupils. But there are differences even here. The aims of high school education are often more difficult to state concretely than those of elementary education. What specifically do we want pupils to learn, for example, from a reading and discussion of Shakespeare's *Julius Caesar?* Lesson plans at this level also include a great deal more about the subject matter to be learned, because the high school teacher is supposed to be something of an expert, at least more so than the elementary teacher.

Although future high school teachers spend much less time in methods courses, they must in fact learn a methodology that is in many ways more varied and complicated than that of the elementary school. The well-trained secondary teacher is at least made familiar with and advised how to manage effectively such instructional techniques as group discussion and debate, brainstorming and buzz-grouping, learning through such "gaming" methods as role-play, the case method, laboratory methods, and many others.

The rest of this chapter samples that wide range of material likely to be found in a secondary methods course, to convey some sense of the techniques to be learned and student activities often required in learning them.

Evaluating High School Textbooks

High school teachers are often given a fair amount of leeway in choosing the texts they prefer to use with their pupils. Their professional college courses aim, therefore, at providing them with skills needed to make judgments about textbooks that are on the market. At the least, college students will be asked to become familiar with reviews, written by experts, of materials in their field; an important course assignment might well consist of doing a thorough evaluation of a text. The excerpts below are taken as an illustration from the analysis of a history text by an expert.[3] An assignment to students might ask them to provide similar answers, though the same level of language would not be required:

> TARGET POPULATION: Grades 10–12; designed for students in Grade 11, but feedback indicates it can be used by students who read at Grade 10 level.
> CURRICULUM ROLE: A two-semester course in American history from pre-history to 1971.
> DEVELOPER'S RATIONALE: To facilitate the acquisition of a knowledge of history through the inquiry method;

to teach history as a means of "knowing ourselves," on the basis that the tasks and skills of historical inquiry can readily be transferred to other intellectual and social applications.

LEARNER GOALS: The program seeks to improve the ability to think independently, to make judgments based on evaluation, to ask probing questions, and to make inferences.

CONGRUENCE: Goals and objectives are well defined and congruent with one another, and suitable for the target population.

SEQUENCE: The sequence suggested by the author is based on a chronological ordering of the material as well as on the building of concepts.

ACCURACY: Analysts note that content was chosen to raise questions in the mind of the readers and to open up discussion about controversial aspects of our nation's past.

FAIRNESS: Analysts advise that authors have conscientiously designed material to avoid stereotypes and racial bias.

METHODOLOGY: There is a detailed teacher's guide prepared for teachers who may be inexperienced in the directed discussion-inquiry mode of instruction. . . . Because the method requires the assistance of a leader or moderator, the material should be used in small groups, if time and space permit. . . . The analysts feel that this material will appeal to teachers who have become disenchanted with coverage as an instructional objective and who are dissatisfied with the lecture as the principal mode of teaching American history.

Using Special Resources

As youngsters reach junior and senior high school, learning aims tend to shift into more remote areas of time and space and higher levels of abstraction. Literature, history, and social studies tend to examine events and ideas that are not a part of the experience of the particular generation of high school youth in the schools. The Korean War of the 1950s is no more "real" to the present-day adolescent than the American Revolution, although most adults who fought in the former conflict are only in their forties and fifties. Both the physical sciences and the social sciences present concepts to be learned that are no longer easy to demonstrate. The boiling point of water can be shown in the early grades by putting a thermometer in a pot of boiling water; learning what "ecology" means is quite another matter.

All professional courses include some treatment of the skills and background needed to successfully introduce media into the classroom: movies, television, trips, outside speakers, illustrations, and other tools for bridging the gap between the learner's experience and what is to be taught. The nature of that gap has itself been illustrated in graphic form in Edgar Dale's "Cone of Experience"—reproduced here in Figure 2— which may be found in many texts in the secondary methods field.

This section of the professional course in some colleges gives students an opportunity to learn how to handle and operate such equipment as 16-mm projectors. Assignments include such activities as:

> Preparing a demonstration or a series of chalkboard materials to accompany a specific lesson plan.
>
> Viewing an instructional film in the student's field and developing a set of guiding questions for a class discussion that would follow a showing of the film in the classroom.
>
> Writing a plan for taking an eleventh grade class on a visit to a local newspaper, including what they will be seeing and hearing on site, and exactly how discussion of the trip will be handled.

Assessing Pupil Progress

In the elementary school, measuring instructional results in the form of tests of pupil progress in reading and arithmetic is usually done by the school system itself. The tests given are likely to be ones that are used nationwide, and that permit a school to compare its own pupils with a national average. At the high school level, because of the great variety of courses and objectives, teachers tend to do some of their own testing. Many secondary teaching programs, therefore, include the skills of evaluating pupil learning by constructing teacher-made tests, as well as interpreting the scores of the standardized tests that high school students often take, such as the reading and mathematics tests used nationally.

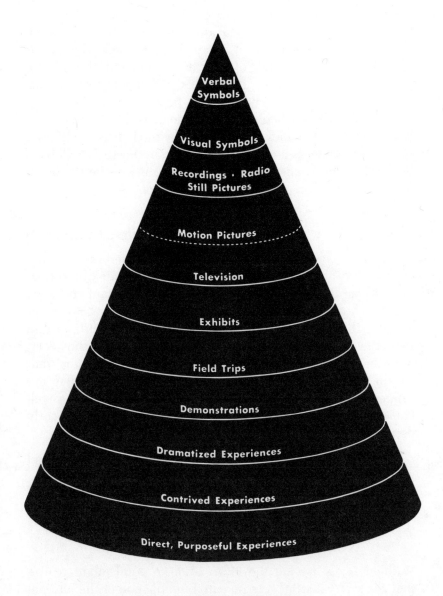

Figure 2. The Cone of Experience

Learning to develop one's own tests is a process that some education majors find fascinating, while others consider it too technical. Many humanist educators think that formal testing is too narrow and mechanical a way of determining what pupils have learned, and schools of education dominated by this approach may require very little skill development in this area. However, the public generally has been showing increasing concern about the schools' ability to demonstrate that children have learned what they should have learned. It is likely, as a result, that students going into education in the 1980s will have to develop some understanding of testing, and of the standards for creating reliable classroom evaluations of pupil growth.

Learning How to Write a Good Multiple-Choice Item

The most efficient, though not necessarily the best, measure of the extent to which pupils have acquired a body of information, or can demonstrate understanding of important concepts, is through objective multiple-choice tests. A fairly large number of such items can be answered in a brief period of time, and they can be scored quickly. A good deal of effort, however, must be devoted to preparing such a test, making sure that wording is clear, and that the questions test what they are supposed to. The techniques for writing good items are well known and not difficult to grasp. For example, here is a poorly designed American history item:

A decisive battle between United States soldiers and American Indians was the
  a. battle called "Custer's last stand"
  b. fighting at Yorktown
  c. War of 1812
  d. storming of the Alamo

Without really having the information, a pupil might realize that the word "battle" was repeated in only one of the alternative answers, and that since a "war" usually involves many battles (and thus must be incorrect), "a" is the answer.

Using Essay Questions Appropriately

Essay questions are thought to be easy to write, and they allow teachers to assess very complicated learning aims, such as pupils' creativity, or their ability to interpret evidence. But essay answers are difficult to evaluate objectively (readers can be misled even by bad handwriting, for example), and take so much time to write that an essay test cannot cover much ground. They are not, in fact, as easy to write as many people think; course work on measurement will help students learn to write effective essay questions, as well as provide techniques for evaluating the essays as objectively as possible.

The reader may by this point appreciate that in the few professional courses usually allotted to the preparation of secondary education teachers an enormous amount of technical material must be included. Each department of education must selectively pick and choose, from a diverse body of materials and information, the knowledge and skills *they think* most important for high school teachers to acquire. College students majoring in a subject with the intention of teaching it at the high school level, therefore, should realize that they may have to fill in some of the gaps themselves.

NOTES

[1] J. Lloyd Trump and Delmas F. Miller, *Secondary School Curriculum Improvement* (Boston: Allyn and Bacon, 1973), p. 351.
[2] Jean Dresden Grambs, John C. Carr, and Robert M. Fitch, *Modern Methods in Secondary Education,* Third Edition (New York: Holt, Rinehart & Winston, 1970).
[3] Educational Products Information Exchange, Report No. 71, pp. 32–33.

5

Student Teaching

First big self-test today! Taught my first class, French II, 12:30 P.M., right after lunch. The morning was hectic, but I was very calm and collected after lunch. I felt strange on the other side of the fence. Last week I could see the teacher's position very clearly, but it's quite a different matter when you get up there and take a look from the other side. Time went by quickly, too, but not quite as fast as I went through my lesson. I finished up all the material I had planned to cover before the period was over. However, I had expected a better response from the class. What I gave them today was supposedly not entirely new material, but they acted as if they had never heard it before. They did cooperate, though—they paid attention and at least tried. I did find that things don't come out as they do when you plan them on paper. . . . Maybe I was too overconfident?[1]

The course work that we have described does not take place entirely in a college classroom. Increasingly it includes some time in schools or in other youth-serving agencies in the community, to give students early experience with the real world of the school and with various settings in which professionals work with children.

Very early in the program, for example, students will probably find themselves in a nearby school for an hour or two a week just observing what goes on, writing reports or reactions, and discussing them with others. A little later, field assignments may very well include acting as an instructional aide for a teacher for a half-day, tutoring pupils who need special attention, helping with some of the clerical chores of the classroom, checking homework assignments, and the like. Finally, toward the end of the college sequence, in one of the semesters during the senior year or possibly for the entire year, students spend a major proportion of their time in a school under the direct supervision of a member of the teaching staff, usually called, in this context, a "cooperating teacher." Student teaching is an experience that most teachers regard as the most valuable part of their professional college training.

Indeed, so valuable is this opportunity to try out teaching skills in a setting in which support is available and mistakes can be turned into a chance to learn, that both teacher trainers and students wish there could be more of it. The minimum number of hours for this apprenticeship is generally in the 250–300 range (five mornings a week for a semester). Because it is expensive to arrange and to supervise, many colleges cannot increase student teaching time beyond that level.

There are some programs, however, that manage to provide something special in practical experiences, and students not yet committed to a college may find it worthwhile to search these programs out. One state university in the Midwest, for example, developed a very interesting semester follow-up to a fairly traditional student teaching semester; they called it the "Elementary Team Internship Program." Those who planned the program saw the need for a kind of training that would fall between the student teacher experience (in which the student seldom gets enough actual teaching time), and the first lonely semester of real teaching, when very little expert guidance is available.

The team internship concept gave the interns real responsibility for their decisions in the classroom by removing the direct presence of a supervising teacher, but kept that teacher available for help when needed. The college instructor was also on tap for conferences when requested.

The team consisted of the following members: four interns, specially selected students who had shown promise during their student teaching semester, two assigned to one classroom together, the other pair to a second classroom; one teacher-director, an experienced teacher in the school in charge of both classes and the four interns; and one college supervisor. Each

73

intern was present for 80 percent of the week, the equivalent of four full days each week for a semester. Because there were two interns to a class, they each taught one day alone, the other days cooperatively. Sinch both classes were "covered" all the time, the teacher-director was able to spend her time planning activities with a single member of one of the teams, or observing one of the classes, or any number of other supervisory and training duties. The college instructor worked closely with the teacher-director and was available to observe, analyze and demonstrate.

Programs of this kind usually generate a good deal of enthusiasm among both interns and college faculty, though, because of their cost, they are by no means common. Interns report much greater feelings of self-confidence as a result of so much independent teaching practice, and a greater willingness to try new ideas. Faculty generally find the internship not only an excellent training tool but one that both parents and staff teachers in the school itself see as useful.

Organization

The average student teaching experience does not, unfortunately, bear much resemblance to this internship model. Students are placed in a school for a period of time running from nine to eighteen weeks, assigned to a particular teacher and classroom. How much actual teaching experience they have in this situation depends largely on the willingness of that cooperating teacher to turn the class over to the student. In addition to assigned classroom activities, students also are encouraged to go along with their cooperating teacher to faculty meetings and other professional activities as they occur normally in the school.

College rules differ on the question of regular academic work permitted during this student teacher period. The number of academic credits allowed is usually at least restricted; total credits seldom may go above twelve, including six to nine credits for student teaching itself. Some college programs permit no additional courses at all.

Groups of student teachers do meet, however, outside their

assigned schools during the clinical semester. At the very least these workshop sessions, usually held on campus but sometimes at a convenient off-campus site, include:

—a preliminary meeting whose major purpose is to orient the students to their new role, including discussions of their responsibilities to the supervising teacher and to the pupils, and the opportunities for learning and growth for themselves

—a meeting some time around mid-semester to give group members an opportunity to exchange teaching experiences and problems, discuss possible solutions for common difficulties, and suggest improvements that can be made during the second half of the term

—a terminal session to help students think about their strengths and weaknesses as revealed by the experience, and to indicate those areas for future development to which they need to pay attention

The college supervisor who works with a small number of students throughout the term may arrange to visit each classroom once a week in school districts where the college has been able to cluster a number of students in a school close to one another. In large cities, where supervisors must spend a good deal of time just getting from one school to the next, visits are likely to be made less often. Supervisors have a difficult and often delicate role to play. They must share the guidance task with each of the cooperating teachers, but at the same time, having the major responsibility for the students, they must make sure that the needs of the students are met.

Both supervisors usually attempt to set up a number of practice experiences for students that gradually provide them with increasing responsibility. For example:

Getting familiar with the pupils in the classroom, looking through their folders and connecting faces with names

Learning about the school itself and its program, what facilities are available, what the community expects of it

Taking the instructional role with small groups of children, or supervising their activities when they are engaged in independent learning activities

75

Taking on a wide range of professional activities, including routines such as arranging bulletin boards, keeping an attendance register, and making daily lesson plans; gradually taking over responsibility for parts of the daily instruction

Student Teacher Comments

The clearest picture of what student teaching is like as an experience is to listen to some reasonably typical reports from students who went through it. Before going on to a more systematic look at the problems students encounter, and what colleges do about them, here are some comments from real student teachers of the recent past, beginning with an entry from a log kept by one of them doing student teaching in a high school:[2]

> After looking forward to it for so long, I started my student teaching. Well, no really—I'll have to wait until next Monday to really get into it. This week I will be observing the classes that I will eventually take over. . . . What a change from the university! These kids are awake and jumping at 8:30 A.M.—and on Monday morning, no less! . . . I found the classroom and was welcomed again by Mrs. B., as I had met her two weeks ago and gotten acquainted. I went through the whole day with Mrs. B. and was introduced to all of her classes. I am worried about having to learn all those names. I carried the seating charts around all day, hoping that eventually the names will all sink in.
>
> At lunch I was introduced to several members of the faculty. Everyone was friendly and interested in my reactions to the school. During the afternoon I received two added bonuses (?) for a first day. I felt I was getting into the routine of things when a bell sounded in the middle of the fifth period. I sat looking startled until someone yelled "fire drill." I got out with the rest of them. After school I saw another school operation—faculty meeting. It wasn't at all like I had pictured. With 150 faculty members it was more like a convention. Things were somewhat unorganized. Some teachers were busy grading papers, small groups were carrying on their own conversations. I found it difficult to take it all in. During this meeting I was introduced to the whole faculty,

and half-dazed, managed to squeak out a few words about myself. After the main meeting I met with the Language Department and received a cordial welcome from all. I was bushed when I got home. The pace seemed very different from my typical day on campus.

Students taking over a class for the first time are usually themselves only a few years out of adolescence. It is very understandable, then, that one of the anxieties uppermost in their minds is whether a group of children are going to be "teachable," that is, orderly and responsive to their instructions. Listen to what some student teachers have said on this issue:[3]

> One aspect of my teaching that hindered me was the fact that I was not forceful enough. That is something that I shall remember when I begin teaching next fall. Discipline is of the greatest importance; without it there can be no learning . . .
>
> My first teaching experience was a very discouraging one. My students found humor in something I had said to them. The class broke into gales of laughter which I could not control. My first experience turned into pure bedlam, and as you can imagine, I went home quite discouraged. But, every day became progressively better . . .
>
> Discipline was one aspect of teaching that really scared me. I have never respected any teacher who did not command discipline in his or her classes. In an unruly atmosphere students learn little when they could be gaining so much from a challenging teacher. If I can't command discipline and respect in my class, I shall not teach.

Many student teachers report rewarding relationships with both their pupils and with the faculty of their schools:

> In my classroom we were at times able to establish something different from the mere teacher-student relationship. Certain projects encouraged a collaborating attitude or feeling. The inner-class relationships were varied, subtle, and often a surprise. I tried to find out what made this class function as a group by various activities. It made an interesting study of how we learn . . .
>
> I was very pleased because the teachers at the school treated me as a fellow teacher and not as a student. I was respected as an equal . . .

It is really amazing how becoming a teacher and associating with experienced teachers in the school situation makes me a part of the professional world . . .

Some of the children began to look on me not only as their teacher but as their friend. Also, some of them were eager to share their treasured secrets with me . . .

And, here, finally, are some overall judgments of the student teacher experience:

Briefly, I enjoyed practice teaching. This surprised me because I was not sure before this experience that I wanted to go into teaching. Most of all, I enjoyed working with children . . .

Now that practice teaching is over, I look back and realize that I did a lot of growing up in eight weeks. I can better control my emotions and better accept my position as a disciplinarian. I have gained understanding. I am still idealistic, but I have learned to live with partial failure while striving for greater success. I still want more than mediocrity, and wonder, "Is my progress enough?" I know that the only way to find out is to give my self a year or two to try my wings. I am not complaining, because teaching has proved to be the challenge I want . . .

It was the most interesting and rewarding experience of my life. In my preparation for teaching, it was the most educational of any encounter I have had. Being in the actual teaching situation gave me more insight into the professional aspect of teaching than any previous experience. It provided an opportunity to evaluate my previous ideas and convictions about the field . . .

Student Teacher Concerns

Several aspects of the student teacher experience are generally perceived to be troublesome. Most of them *are* sources of difficulty because this period in their life is one in which their own lives are changing: from student to independent adult, from study to work and a career, from being dependent on others to a role reversal—having children depend on them.

It is easy to see why, at such a time, self-doubt is so common,

78

and a fear of being unable to measure up to the demands of the new role as teacher should strike so many. Students' concern about their own abilities can itself create problems in student teaching, because it may lead students to an overemphasis on the approval of others. Comments such as those quoted earlier on how difficult it is to impose discipline on children are often an outgrowth of that need. In an attempt to get children's approval, student teachers find it difficult to enforce school regulations, or to insist on the learning standards the school expects its teachers to maintain. Because student teachers are still playing the student role in their own colleges, they may find it tempting to be on the side of the children as they develop friendships with them. This has become even more tempting in recent years as some professionals in education, social work, and other caretaking fields have stressed what they call a "child advocate" role.

But, being an "advocate" for the needs of children under one's care, as desirable as it may seem, is a very complicated and difficult role to play when the professionals must also represent the adult system that hires them, and to which they owe their primary allegiance. And, if the cooperating teacher presents a desirable teacher-role model, their own future growth as professionals should lead student teachers to identify with their supervisors, rather than with the children. One study of junior high school student teachers found that their children rated them as more friendly and vigorous than their regular teachers, but also as less firm. This suggests that, whether it is desirable or not, student teachers do tend to follow the pattern just described.

One frequently disconcerting feature of most student teaching experiences is the written evaluation or "mark" given the student teacher by the school supervising teacher. Such a judgment might well be an unhappy but accurate measure of student teachers' ability in the real situation, in contrast to their verbal, academic ability. But it might also reflect a difference between local standards for teaching in the school system in which students are performing their student teaching stint and the standards taught in the university, or even a personality clash between two generations or two persons with different values. Student teachers should appreciate the advantage in

79

finding out on what basis and upon what criteria they are going to be judged even before they begin the student teaching experience.

The rating scale presented in Figure 3 is a good example of the type of scale often used to judge student teacher performance—one that indicates very clearly the standards to which students are to be held. The person making the judgment indicates a rating for each specific item; the rating is then multiplied by a factor that represents the relative importance of each group of items.

The reader might wish to find out some of the problems involved in any rating scale of this kind by filling it out, along with a fellow student, as a rating of a teacher both have had in the past. A comparison of the two ratings is likely to show at least some differences.

The Cooperating Teacher

Adjusting to the teacher's role in the classroom and learning to overcome your own psychological conflicts in relation to the children, are only part of the strain of student teaching. Some of the rest is generated in the developing relationships with the important others involved in the experience: those who instruct, help, judge and criticize, and, sometimes, cause student teachers a good deal of anguish.

Cooperating teachers are supposed to be models for their students, and many studies of student teachers show that it often turns out that way, that students tend to end the semester imitating their supervising teacher to a significant degree. But many problems can arise, and which ones a student teacher will encounter is part of the "luck of the draw." For example, not all teachers who are put into the supervisory position have the natural ability to deal sympathetically with young and uncertain students, to correct their mistakes diplomatically, to know when assistance is needed and when it is better to let students deal with their own problems. Some of these problems in human relations are noted mockingly in the following Ten Commandments for cooperating (supervising) teachers devised by a college coordinator of student teaching programs:[4]

80

Student's Name_____ Trait for Evaluation	Poor 1	Average 2	Good 3	Weight	Total
Ability to develop pupil's self-control				2.5	
Personal influence					
Ability to teach how to study					
Enthusiasm					
Ability to stimulate thinking					
Skill in questioning					
Ability to discipline					
Ability to motivate students					
Definite aim					
Care of individual needs					
Ability to develop good habits				2.0	
Ability to understand the learner					
Attention to responses of pupils					
General growth					
Adaptability					
Skill in making assignments					
Interest in pupils					
Ability to organize subject matter					
Growth in subject					
Cheerfulness					
Ability to be tactful					
Choice of subject matter					
Practice of self-control					
Ability to be sympathetic				1.5	
Sincerity					
Sense of justice					
Attention to health of pupils					
Daily preparation					
Initiative, self-reliance					
Ability to cooperate					
Professional interest					
Attention to punctuality of pupils					
Sense of humor					
Accuracy					
Industry					
Interest in school					
Grasp of subject matter					
Care of routine					
Attention to neatness of room					
Promptness with reports					
Interest in community				1.0	
Punctuality, attendance					
Intellectual capacity					
Posture					
Voice					
Use of English					
Care of light, heat, ventilation					
Economy of using material					
Dress					
Health					

Total Index

Figure 3. Weighted Rating Scale for Teachers

From *The Student Teacher in the Secondary School* by Lester D. Crow and Alice Crow. Copyright © 1964 by Longman Inc. Reprinted by permission of Longman.

1. Thou shalt remember that thy student teacher is inexperienced and lacking in teaching aids with which to teach thy students unless thou shareth thine own with him.

2. Thy student teacher is frail and easily overburdened by too many classes assigned too soon, yet surely he needeth practice to grow in stature.

3. Thou shalt not attempt to mould thy fledgling in thy image, for he hath a personality different from thine.

4. Thou shalt not shame or reproach thy student teacher by saying, "Verily, thou didst not profit from thy campus disciplines as did my student teacher before thee, for he was richly blessed with initiative and imagination."

5. Thou shouldst hide the light of thy excellence under thy humility in order that the light from the student teacher should fill the classroom, for it is surely a blessing to train one whose skill excells thine own.

6. When thou commandeth thy student teacher saying, "Go forth and prepare a lesson plan for the morrow;" and he returneth forthwith, be not hasty in discarding the ideas therein lest he raise his voice in lamentation saying, "I am exceedingly sad and sorrowful for, lo, I am permitted no experimenting."

7. Thou should not always refuse when thy student teacher wishes to depart from thy established way, neither should thou remain steadfastly in thy room at all times, nor tarry in the teacher's lounge at great length.

8. When thou discovereth a weakness in thy student teacher, thou shalt confer with him privily to show him the error of his way while there is yet time for improvement.

9. When the student teacher lags in his progress, thou shalt make him mindful of his slowness and show him how his stride may be lengthened and his pace quickened.

10. Thou shalt not use much flowery praise to lead thy student teacher to believe he doeth well and then cast him down with thy mark and thy recommendation.

Although schools of education have some influence on the selection of supervisory teachers, the cooperating schools have a good deal to say about it. Principals are apt to choose wisely, but, in a number of cases and for a variety of reasons, students may confront a supervisor without enough teaching experience to be a very valuable guide and helper. Even if cooperating teachers are competent and experienced teachers, they may have little experience at the task of supervision. As a result, they may take refuge in filling the student teacher's days with menial tasks simply out of their own insecurity.

The other side of that coin is that the supervisor is so confident of his or her own teaching methods that students are not permitted to develop their own style and to experiment with themselves as teachers. Directly or indirectly, such supervisors say, "Forget all that baloney about teaching that they taught you in your college courses, because you're in the real world now and you'd better do things my way, the right way."

The College Supervisor

The student, the cooperating teacher, and the college supervisor form a trio that sometimes increases or exceeds the difficulties in the two-way relationship just described. The college representatives are the key persons in the three-way relationship because they are more experienced and knowledgeable about education (usually) than the supervising teacher, and bear the responsibility for the training of their students.

Unfortunately, their own responsibilities, limitations and restraints often do not permit the college representatives to be as effective as everyone would wish them to be. They usually have too many students to supervise and cannot command the resources in their college or department to maximize their function as ideal mentors. Instead of being free to concentrate on the problems of maintaining a difficult three-way human relationship, they may be overwhelmed by details and routines, tired of daily travel from one school to another, and caught in the occasional conflicts between student and supervising teacher.

Some of the problems that arise are simply an unavoidable part of the situation itself. For one thing, two members of the trio come from one institution, the college, and the third is a member of another system. Some misunderstanding and conflict, in such a case, can be expected. No one in this tripartite relationship, furthermore, has very much free choice in the nature or structure of the relationship. The college supervisor is usually given a list of students to supervise and schools in which the students have already been placed. The cooperating teachers may or may not have the right to accept or refuse a student teacher, but even if they have the right they have little information to go on about the student. Student teachers themselves, of course, are even more at the mercy of the situation. They may have a choice of grade level, and possibly something to say about the school in which they will student-teach, but very little control over anything else.

Some students, of course, may happen upon a very good student teaching situation, and for them the view just sketched will seem a very pessimistic one. But it can be expected to be more or less realistic for many. Although there is not very much information available in the wide variety of student teaching situations that exist around the country, one study that closely observed the experience of about 125 student teachers discovered two particularly significant features.[5]

One was that an alliance forms between the college supervisor and the cooperating teacher, in which each develops a positive relationship with the other, and both have a rather negative relationship with the student. It's not difficult to understand why this happens so frequently, since the two supervisors share common background features such as age and educational experience. Both of them also are being judged by others, in the school and in the college, on the basis of how well their pupil is performing.

Nor, given this pattern, is it hard to understand the study's second finding—that as the semester or year wears on, the relationship between the three persons becomes less positive. That is, by the end of the student teaching period, the three people involved are less interested in spending time with one another, and find less value than before in the relationship generally.

There are some consolations, however, for student teachers. One is that they are not alone—almost all training periods known to man in which professionals must test their new skills in a supervised field experience have many of the same difficulties. And, as an earlier part of this chapter pointed out, there are many rewarding features to the experience that make up for the problems, and student teachers can usually also find several sources of support, to help them deal with problems as they appear. There is often more than one student teacher assigned to the same school, which provides the possibility for peer support that can be genuinely helpful. Most students have also found, by this time in the education sequence, a member of the college faculty they like and trust, and to whom they can turn for some confidential advice.

Resources

In addition to the actual time spent in the classroom, and in addition to discussions with the cooperating teacher and the college supervisor based on the experience there, students will have available to them a range of more academic aids—from textbooks written specifically for student teachers to special seminars in which groups of student teachers meet regularly to analyze their experiences. So great are the differences in colleges around the country that it would be misleading to try to describe any pattern of resources as common or typical. One can only describe a few of them as illustrative.

If the education program assigns any textbook at all to its student teachers, however, it is not likely to be startlingly different from other texts written for the same purpose. The topics below are reasonably representative of most texts for secondary school student teachers; most of them may also be found in the elementary school equivalents.

Preparatory Information and Advice

Expectations and anxieties of students; what to look for in a visit to the school before the program begins; services you can depend on from the college.

Establishing Relationships

Working with the cooperating teacher: types of difficulties often encountered, needed skills in human relations; whom to go to when in trouble; the need for prudence in going through channels; factors affecting the student teacher role, and how to deal with conflict within the role.

Working with pupils: discussion of the kind of relationship with children that is most productive to build; general principles of classroom management; learning to work with your cooperating teacher's concept of classroom discipline.

Learning about the school and the community: discovering the philosophy of the school; relations with other faculty members; finding out where special resources of the school are and how to use them; getting information about the community; learning how to talk with typical parents of that communtiy.

Being a Teacher

Planning lessons and other learning experiences; selecting and using materials; building effective learning situations; evaluating pupil progress.

Special Issues

Evaluating your own work and your own growth; developing a personal code of ethics.

Your future in the profession: how to go about finding your first position; requirements for advancement toward a variety of professional goals.

Seminar discussions focus on many of these same topics, but where possible, they use actual classroom incidents described by student participants. Many colleges also involve cooperating teachers in a seminar at the college to help them develop more skill at their supervisory task. Sometimes these sessions can be given focus by using case materials developed for this purpose. The case reproduced below illustrates the types of problems both cooperating and student teachers face daily in their relationship:[6]

> As he rode to school, Ross Whittaker was thinking about yesterday's class discussion in his student teaching seminar. Mr. Bailey, his supervisor, had talked about the importance of various kinds of records and reports. He had particularly

urged the students to look over the cumulative records of the children in their classrooms.

Ross had been in a fourth grade class for two weeks, and there were a few children whose records he was particularly anxious to read. There was Betsy, for instance, who almost never spoke; and Donald, who became upset so easily. Ross decided to read their records as soon as possible.

He arrived in the classroom just as Mrs. Curten, the teacher, was hanging up her coat. After their good mornings, Ross said, "Say, Mrs. Curten, I'd like to look at some of the children's folders and read their records today."

"Why, Ross," replied Mrs. Curten, "what a request! We never show those folders to anyone. You ought to know that records are extremely confidential, and that only the teachers have access to them."

COMMENTS

Should confidential information such as children's records be shared with student teachers? Is a student to be regarded as a professional co-worker, a college Junior or Senior, or a person somewhere in between?

And how should the differing opinions of a college supervisor and a cooperating teacher be dealt with? The student is usually caught in the middle. How may Mrs. Curten react if Ross informs her his college supervisor told him to look at the children's records?

NOTES

[1] Jean D. Grambs, John C. Carr, Robert M. Fitch, *Modern Methods in Secondary Education,* 3d ed. (New York: Holt, Rinehart & Winston, 1970), p. 21.

[2] Ibid., p. 16.

[3] William Sezak, "Student Teaching: The Shakedown Cruise," Lowell Horton and Phyllis Horton, *Teacher Education, Trends, Issues, Innovations* (Danville, Ill.: Interstate Printers, 1974), pp. 227–33.

[4] Leonard Douglas, "Ten Commandments for Cooperating Teachers," from *Kappa Delta Pi Record,* December 1967, p. 49. Used with permission of Mrs. Bonnie Douglas.

[5] Albert H. Yee, "Interpersonal Relationships in the Student-Teaching Triad," *Journal of Teacher Education,* Spring 1968, pp. 95–112.

[6] Elizabeth Hunter, *The Cooperating Teacher At Work, Case Studies of Critical Incidents* (New York: Holt, Rinehart & Winston, 1962), p. 35.

6

Undergraduate Specialization

Specialized educational fields first appeared as academic or vocational concentrations in the high school; the elementary school dealt generally with the "common branches," with all teachers giving instruction in all subjects: language arts, arithmetic, and social studies. Now specializations are beginning to appear in the elementary grades as well.

It is not too difficult to find special teaching positions in elementary schools in art, music, mathematics, or reading. Teachers who have these jobs do not have a group of their own pupils, but take over the other teachers' classes for a period or two a week, or work with special groups of pupils who may leave their own classrooms to form a new group for a given period of time during the day or the week. Students considering a major in education should investigate opportunities for making use of a special talent or a particular interest in increasingly available special majors that combine teacher preparation with an academic field such as art.

This chapter will explore a different kind of specialization, the kind that has developed in response to the special educational needs of particular groups of children. There are a number of such groups that are now establishing their right to special treatment from the schools, and we will concentrate on the three most important of them: the very young, the handicapped, and the non-English speaking. Although most of the specialized programs that prepare teachers to meet the special needs of these children are still restricted to the master's degree level, special courses are increasingly offered to undergraduates. Other emerging specializations, such as teaching the gifted child, are seldom available at the undergraduate level at all, and are difficult to find even in graduate programs, because the demand for them is as yet too small.

Early Childhood

Until the middle of this century our public school systems paid very little attention to early childhood. In the days when only a small minority of married women worked at regular jobs outside the home, the early development of children was assumed to be the mother's responsibility. Even as late as 1964, only about one out of every four children between the ages of three and five were enrolled in some form of schooling. Ten years later that proportion had doubled, and half of all children at that age were in some form of nursery school or kindergarten.

Such a very recent surge in numbers, however, does not mean that the whole idea of early childhood education is new; the interest in schooling the very young child has, in fact, a respectably long history, beginning in the seventeenth century in the works of John Amos Comenius. A century after that the French philosopher, Rousseau, whose ideas have also had an enormous influence on modern intellectual thought in general, wrote a book about how he would raise an imaginary child— an education that would begin at birth. In *Émile*, Rousseau emphasizes the importance of the early years, a theme that was quickly picked up by a number of other European educators, who set up some model schools for preschool youngsters. These models followed Rousseau's ideas of teaching children primarily through the sense of touch, sight, and hearing rather than through words, his emphasis on a natural environment of fields and growing things, and the importance of play. These notions gradually evolved into the kindergarten ("children's garden") of the twentieth-century elementary school.

But only some of the very large number of U.S. children in early childhood programs are in kindergarten—the year that immediately precedes first grade. The rest are in one or another of a wide variety of nursery schools and day care centers, some of which are private, other publicly funded and operated.

This very rapid growth of the early childhood field is due only in part to the increase in the number of working mothers. Educators and the public generally are concerned about the difficulties that many minority youngsters are having in school, and the idea of beginning early with the task of preparing them for school has become very appealing. "Head Start," a comprehensive federal program for very young disadvantaged children, began in the middle 1960s and has become one of the most popular of all the federal antipoverty programs. It is comprehensive in the sense that its three- and four-year-old clients are provided not only with instruction in reading and number readiness, but with health and nutritional services, and family help as well.

Many of the programs considered to be a part of early childhood are operated entirely apart from regular schools. Head Start, for example, has its own centers; many of the private nursery schools are run by churches and other nonschool agencies. It is possible that in the long run most of these activities will be taken over by the public schools, but for a time, at least, students interested in working with very young children have a great variety of different settings to consider. And, in this rapidly growing field, there are many kinds of early-childhood teacher training programs available as well.

Teacher Training for Early Childhood

Some teacher training programs specialize to such an extent that they provide very little *but* early childhood; at the other extreme, students may be required to major in elementary education generally, and find only a few courses aimed specifically at the early childhood field. The more typical option is a well-structured series of courses available as a subspecialty within an elementary sequence. Even the student who feels committed to early childhood as a professional field should think carefully about choosing too specialized a program. Many states (Alabama, Connecticut, and Florida, for example) do not issue or recognize an early childhood license as such, and in such states a pure early childhood specialization may certify students for nursery school or Head Start centers, but not for kindergarten teaching in the regular public schools.

In any event, early childhood programs basically follow much the same curriculum that was earlier described for the elementary sequence, including developmental psychology, learning, social influences on development, specific curriculum areas, and instructional techniques. They simply involve a greater (even exclusive) concentration on the early years of the child, and on a few specific topics with which only the early childhood specialists need to concern themselves.

Early Childhood Settings. Just as the student preparing to teach in the elementary grades is provided with a kind of map of the elementary school as an organization, so the early childhood teacher-to-be is introduced to various types of early childhood programs. We have already mentioned a few of them, but all of the following settings are likely to be surveyed in some depth:

Nursery schools. These are considered to be the first of the series of units that make up the elementary school, and some regular schools already include a nursery school year (for four-year-olds) as a step before kindergarten. Private nursery schools, which are often not attached to an elementary school at all, usually provide a two-year sequence for three-and four-year-olds.

Kindergarten. The well-established first year of elementary school, for five-year-olds.

Child development centers. A general term for Head Start-like centers for disadvantaged children, this type of setting includes a classroom and a play area, and is devoted to bringing together resources of both the family and the community to help in the development of the young child.

Schools for exceptional children. The early childhood section of special schools, for either especially gifted children or those handicapped mentally, physically, or emotionally. A later section of this chapter will deal with this kind of special education.

Coop nursery school. Usually organized by families who cannot afford regular private nurseries, these are cooperative ventures in which a number of parents pool their funds and contribute their own time, along with a person qualified in early childhood education.

Day care centers. These often put their emphasis on just taking care of children while their mothers work, but many of them also have an educational component.

Play schools. Usually operated by a church or a neighborhood organization.

Early Child Development. Some college programs merely add an emphasis on early growth within child development or child psychology courses, but more highly specialized programs provide a separate course on the preschool years. In this course considerable attention is usually given to important figures in early childhood psychology such as Maria Montessori, on the basis of whose theories a number of early childhood schools still operate. Students of the field are also expected to understand in some detail the way in which a wide variety of important skills and abilities mature in the typical child, and, in particular, various theories of how language develops.

Courses of this kind almost always include a series of field experiences involving observations in both nursery schools and kindergartens, and a good deal of emphasis is put on training students to interpret samples of child behavior. For example, a one-paragraph text book description of an episode involving three children playing in a sand enclosure, and the intervention of their teacher, may be followed by a typical set of questions: What can be learned about the maturation, growth, learning, and development of normal three-year-olds from the above incident? Do these observations agree with summary findings of research intended to discover the characteristics of normal three-year-olds? Did the teacher act wisely in terms of the implications of established research findings?

Curriculum. Few of us are used to thinking of such a formidable word as "curriculum" in connection with very young children, but in this field it is used for structured activities with children as young as six months. And one has only to watch toddlers playing with some sophisticated educational toys to realize that skills can be learned from manipulating a well-designed object. Texts in the field usually discuss early childhood activities and experiences in the same curriculum cate-

93

gories we have used earlier: language arts, mathematics, social studies, science, values. Here, for example, are some social studies concepts considered appropriate for the preschooler:

We are not all alike.
Respect for rules and regulations is important.
Money can be used to buy things that are useful to us.
One should not waste resources, like water and food.
People do different kinds of work.
Time relationships exist.
Our society changes.
Weather affects how we live and where we play.

Much of the emphasis in early childhood curriculum, however, is likely to be on some of the special concerns of the field. Some illustrations of these are:

1. A continuation of the traditional interest of the field in the self concept of young children, and in its healthy development, but an increasing concern for early cognitive development, the growth of mental functions. Students are likely to be confronted with a good deal of lively argument over the question of how far this concern should be taken; most early childhood experts, for example, deplore the interest of some educators in teaching two-year-olds to read.

2. Within the very large segment of the field that is primarily concerned with disadvantaged children, the poor and minorities, there has been a good deal of exploration of the usefulness of work with children even before they reach their first birthday (though *not* with the intention of teaching them to read). The theory underlying this movement suggests that the gaps in the experience of disadvantaged children, such as learning to use adults as resources, are responsible for their difficulty in adjusting to the demands of school, and must be compensated for very early in the child's life.

3. There is a continuing and increasing concern for involving parents in the objectives of the school, both at home and within the school itself. So the training of the early childhood teacher, as opposed to other teachers, is likely to involve to a much greater extent the skills needed in working with parents. In many early childhood settings parents work with teachers

on advisory committees, as classroom and playground aides, and as teachers.

Teaching the Mentally Retarded

Special education is the term most commonly used to cover a wide variety of efforts to meet the educational needs of children who are not well served by the typical school situation. It has recently come to include special efforts such as interdisciplinary curriculum development for such exceptional children as the academically gifted and for children abundantly endowed with other talents. For the most part, however, special education refers to those with some kind of handicap: the mentally retarded, the physically impaired (the deaf, the blind, etc.), and the emotionally disturbed.

Professional educators have been concerned about these children for well over a century, and special programs and separate institutions to deal with their problems of development have grown substantially over the twenty-five-year period from 1950 to 1975. These efforts early came to the attention of the general public through the work of such giants in the field as Helen Keller. Considerably more attention will be given to these children in the future because federal legislation has put them very much in the spotlight by making new demands on the schools.

Recent federal law and regulations have changed the schools' relation to these children in several major ways. First, they have made the local school district responsible for the education of *all* children in the district, instead of allowing the states to parcel out primary responsibility to a variety of institutions such as mental hospitals or centers for the retarded. Although districts may arrange for separate care for some children outside the schools, they cannot simply send them to an institution and forget about them. They must monitor their treatment and take responsibility for changes in placement where necessary or desirable. Second, and most important for teachers, the new handicapped-child law requires school districts to "mainstream" as many handicapped children as possible, that is, to place them at least part of the time in the regular classroom.

Students considering teaching careers must take these developments into account. Although many training programs for special education teachers are restricted to the master's degree level, they are increasingly being developed for undergraduates. During the 1970s, as the number of available teaching positions fell, special education was the single field in which they actually increased. Students with some interest in working with the handicapped can check college catalogs for a program that will provide them with this early specialization.

But those who do not share this interest will also be affected. The mainstreaming requirement is changing the pupil mix—in the elementary school in particular—and making the task of the teacher at that level more varied and more complicated. Teacher training is also adapting to these new needs, and is beginning to include the special understanding and the skills required to deal effectively with these children. In the past, the separate schools to which handicapped children were assigned provided young teachers with the opportunity to take on challenging positions while gaining experience that could easily lead to specialized careers. Such separation of handicapped children from the regular school setting is unlikely to survive the many court tests it is now facing.

As an example of the course work typical of the field, and of the kind of material that will be found increasingly in the regular teacher training programs, we have chosen to outline briefly some of the content of a series of courses designed to prepare teachers of the mentally retarded child.

Educating the Mentally Retarded

The educational foundation elements of this special field heavily emphasize the problems involved in testing and developing classification for the retarded. Some experts argue that the term "mental retardation" itself should be done away with, that it stigmatizes those who may well be socially competent enough to live a reasonably independent life, even if they cannot learn all the school now asks them to learn. The term *general learning disabilities* has been proposed as a substitute, but whatever the terminology, students in all fields of education will be required increasingly to learn in some detail the basic elements of what is known about the various classifications of this disability. In brief:

Mildly retarded ("slow learners"), with a measured IQ of about 55–70: Usually unidentified as disabled before school entry, because they seem only a little slower than other children of the same age. These children are capable of learning academic skills that fall between the third and sixth grade; thus they can learn to read and write at a minimal level. As adults, though they may need some guidance, they are capable of considerable independence.

Moderately retarded ("educable mentally retarded"), IQ of about 35–50: Noticeably slower in developing, attain minimal toilet training in early childhood, but do learn to walk and feed themselves. School learning is typically limited to third grade skills or below. As adults, they are capable of unskilled work in sheltered situations, but usually need some supervision throughout life.

Severely retarded, IQ of about 20–35: May learn to walk and feed themselves before six, but very minimal achievement of other self-help skills such as toilet training or speaking. Capable of only the most elementary learning of nonacademic skills, and, as adults, require permanent care.

Profoundly retarded, IQ below 20 or 25: Many are permanently bound to bed, though some may be capable of learning self-feeding skills and have some ability to move about. Never learn to speak and require permanent nursing care.

Mentally retarded children constitute about 2 percent of the school-age population, but the problems they pose for educators are formidable. Students will confront in the foundation courses not only arguments about how valid the above categories are, but debates about the acceptability and usefulness of intelligence tests generally, how limited the learning ability of the retarded is, and a host of other issues about which people in and out of the field disagree.

Here, for example, is a typical attack on the testing that is such a prominent feature of special education:[1]

> Perhaps the most glaring inadequacy of using standard IQ tests with MRs (mental retardates) is that the tests were never standardized for use with retarded persons. Most of

97

the standard tests were devised for use with children or adults of either "normal" or "superior" intelligence. Then it was assumed that children or adults who fall below an arbitrary point were "mentally retarded." But it is obviously impossible to say that a person is mentally retarded when the only proof is a single performance on a test. No valid test, standard or otherwise, has yet been developed or devised for a person of low intelligence so as to determine what constitutes mental retardation. Without a test specifically designed for MRs and without data derived from control groups, no significant assessment of the MR's intelligence is possible.

Many—perhaps the majority—of professional psychologists would disagree with this statement, but it accurately represents the beliefs of a number of persons in teaching and administrative positions in the field.

Curriculum. A number of the questions that students will examine about the curriculum in this area are closely related to the testing and classification controversies described above. Many special educators contend, since they do not trust the tests and diagnostic procedures commonly used, that retarded children are not given an appropriate curriculum. So, for example, if children are mistakenly classified as "severely retarded" they will not be expected to learn at all, when in fact they may be capable of at least minimal attainment of academic skills. Or, they insist, many children are put into separate classes for the educable mentally retarded when they could get along at least minimally in a normal curriculum, if their classroom teacher knows how to deal with their problems skillfully.

A number of state and big city school systems have worked out very detailed plans and objectives for the retarded, at least for the first two categories of disability described earlier. The Illinois Plan, for example, specifies ten curriculum areas as necessary for every mentally retarded child who can be handled within the school system itself:[2]

citizenship
communications
home and family
leisure time
management of materials and money

98

occupational adequacy
physical and mental health
safety
social adjustment
travel

Each of these areas is detailed in the state plan in the form of specific learning objectives at three levels: primary, intermediate, and advanced. In the "home and family" area, for example, children learn the value of cooperation within a family unit. They are taught homemaking skills at a level appropriate to their understanding, and are provided with information about the process of having a family and financing family life.

In recent years a major emphasis on occupational competence for the retarded has developed. In curricula that attempt to implement this notion, basic reading and writing skills are taught by concentrating on letter writing, job hunting, the completion of application and social security forms, using dictionaries and telephone directories, talking on the telephone, and so on. Arithmetic is taught through budgeting, buying, understanding payroll deductions, and making rent payments. Social studies might include surveys of available jobs and taking on the responsibility of citizenship through voting and other activities. Science would examine safety on the job, good health habits, and conventional dating behavior.

Teaching Methods. Although teaching the retarded may be a great deal more of a strain than instructing a normal group, and while it requires at the very least considerable patience, teaching techniques used with retarded children have been much more specifically worked out than those for the regular classroom. Students training for special education, therefore, can often get a much clearer idea of what they must do. For example a major objective with young MRs is to have them acquire the ability to follow simple oral directions. A typical set of instructions for education students includes:[3]

1. Body parts. Begin with singular forms only. Later add plural forms and, later still, randomly mix singular and plural forms: "Touch your ear (eye, nose, head). Touch your ears, (eyes, knees, toes)."

2. Music format. Combine body-part directions with a simple melody such as "Put Your Finger in the Air."
3. Self-introductions. Introduce the children individually to themselves in a full length mirror. "That is Gary Peel. Say 'Hello Gary.' Hold out your hand to the boy in the mirror. What is he doing? Put your hand on your head, your shoulder; touch your nose. Does he do everything you do?"

Or, here is another game that involves auditory decoding, motor encoding, and visual decoding, all of them very basic skills:

Choose a child to be the messenger boy and whisper a "message" to him. He chooses a child to receive the message and whispers the message to this child. Sample messages: "Take off one shoe." "Turn around three times." "Stand on one foot." The child who receives the message acts out the request. The other children then guess out loud what they thought the message was. When the children master the game, they can make up their own messages and you will not need to initiate the messages.

A major technical innovation in the instruction of the mentally retarded at all levels is called *behavior modification,* or sometimes *behavior shaping.* This technique is fairly easily mastered and can be an enormously useful tool for any teacher.

Behavior mod depends on several basic assumptions. One is that important tasks can be broken down into very small units of behavior. (Tying one's shoelace has been analyzed, for MR training purposes, into over five hundred separate behaviors, as one example.) A second assumption, for which there is a great deal of experimental evidence, is that if learners are rewarded fairly soon after producing the behavior, the behavior will tend to occur again—that is, it will be learned.

Behavior mod, and other techniques such as computer teaching, are part of a rapidly growing body of knowledge about how to handle the concrete problems of educating the retarded. Students with an interest in working with these children can depend these days on getting a good deal of help in developing the necessary skills.

Bilingual Education

A very prominent feature of the educational scene, in all parts of the country where substantial numbers of non-English speaking children are to be found, is some form of bilingual/bicultural schooling. Like other specializations, teacher training for bilingual programs is found in some colleges only at the graduate level, but is increasingly becoming a part of undergraduate teacher training.

Since the first large waves of immigration to this country in the mid-nineteenth century, U.S. schools have had to deal with sizeable groups of non-English speaking children. In a nation that took pride in its ability to turn many different nationalities into Americans in a great "melting pot," school policy was to teach non-English-speaking children the language of the country as soon as possible.

During the 1960s this policy came under vigorous attack, and the idea of a bilingual/bicultural school developed. Most of the earlier European immigrants to this country had adopted English as their language; only a tiny percentage of them still spoke their native languages. But there was a very rapidly growing population of Spanish-speaking people who, by the 1970s, numbered about twelve million; about half of this very sizeable group spoke English very poorly or not at all. Many of them did not wish to give up their own culture and language, and blamed the difficulty their children had in U.S. schools on the single-language policy of the schools.

Where some form of special assistance was provided it usually took the form of particular attention to developing English language competency, in an approach called English as a Second Language (ESL). This was thought to be inadequate by many experts, who advocated programs in which children would be taught in their native language until they developed real ability to speak English. They would then be gradually phased into a monolingual English program. Some programs went much further than this: they consisted of an entire twelve years of a curriculum, taught in both the native language and English, and that also included an emphasis on native culture —history, literature, etc.

Beginning in 1968, Congress provided funds for the support of such bilingual programs, and available federal funding has increased substantially through the years. Many states have passed their own laws requiring some form of bilingual schooling for *any* group of non-English speaking children, and the federal education department as well as some federal courts have recognized a constitutional right to such assistance, in order to equalize educational opportunity. Some idea of the number and diversity of non-English-speaking children is conveyed by the following breakdown identified in California schools alone in the middle 1970s: 883 Chinese, 77 French, 62 German, 221 Italian, 450 Japanese, 400 Portuguese, 20 Russian, 39,570 Spanish, 600 Filipino. Over 158,000 others in California of the same ethnic groups were found to speak only limited English!

Teacher training for bilingual positions in the schools is particularly appropriate for fluent native speakers of any language spoken by some reasonably large number of children in U.S. schools. This currently includes Spanish, of course, but also a variety of Asian languages, Italian, French and Portuguese. But, English monolinguals also have a place in the bilingual education picture, because most programs include at least some form of ESL, which can be taught by someone who does not speak the pupils' language.

Curriculum

One primary curriculum issue in bilingual education concerns the differences in program types already mentioned. That is, should non-English-speaking children be taught in their own language only until they have mastered English, or should we encourage the full-scale bilingual/bicultural model? The first of these has come to be called *transitional* bilingual, the second *maintenance* bilingual. The congressional intention in providing funding for the first program was to encourage the easiest possible transition to an English-speaking classroom. Many advocates of multi-ethnic education, such as the U.S. Civil Rights Commission, prefer a continuous bilingual experience throughout schooling because it offers the greatest hope that children will retain their own culture and speech.

Other curriculum issues abound, providing a diverse series of problems for study and analysis in the specialized courses in this field. For example, how should we determine which pupils ought to be admitted to bilingual classes? It seems on the surface to be a simple enough matter to decide who can and who cannot speak English, but like many educational issues, the matter turns out to be quite complicated. There are no very trustworthy tests; some cities, like New York, which is under a court order to develop a bilingual program, determined entry into the program with a test that no one thinks is very good. Thus, some local Spanish groups have protested that pupils think the test is a joke, and that they become so familiar with it by taking it twice a year that many can "graduate" from the program even though they are not very proficient in English.

On the other side of the coin, many of those who prefer a quick transitional program, believe that children with a perfectly adequate mastery of English are admitted into bilingual classes in order to make the program seem more important. The claim is also made that parents, many of whom would rather see their children learn English as quickly as possible, are not given a clear enough choice between bilingual and regular classes. In a number of school systems, for example, children are bureaucratically selected for and placed into bilingual classes unless their parents write specifically asking for their assignment to a regular class.

Teaching Methodologies

Through some years of use in multi-ethnic programs, a number of general teaching strategies have become rather well accepted, and form the specialized topping on the basic teaching methods for general classrooms.

A major emhpasis in all such programs, for example, is on the enhancement of the children's self concept. Most bilingual educators believe that the traditional way of handling non-English-speaking children in school resulted in making them ashamed of their own language and of their own cultural behaviors in a way that sometimes set them apart from other children. They argue that children who do not see themselves as worthy will not learn as well as others. Hence all preparation in methods for

103

teachers in bilingual programs includes insistence that teachers find ways to communicate respect for the children's cultural background, and that they believe the children will succeed at the tasks set for them. So, for example, teachers are trained to refrain from such comments as "Speak loudly so everyone can hear you," until pupils demonstrate that they have gained confidence and ease in the class.

Achieving a positive self and cultural image can also be furthered by careful choice of books for the classroom library, and by the display in the classroom of pictures and artifacts relating to cultural heritage. Teachers are also encouraged to use a Polaroid to take pictures of class activities and individual children, and use the photos to motivate oral and writing activities.

English reading instruction is a major curriculum emphasis, and special bilingual approaches and methods have undergone substantial development. The future teacher might well be asked to master some of the most common of the linguistic differences (and the learning problems they create) between standard English and such languages as Spanish and Chinese. Some vowel sounds, for example, will be difficult for the Spanish-speaking child, as those in "bit," "bat," or "full." The Spanish language does not use some sounds at all, as the *v* in vote or *z* in zoo. Grammatical differences include some uses of negative forms (he no go home), and the order of adjectives (the cap red is pretty). Chinese-speaking people are used to fewer vowels than in English, and a number of English consonants are not found in Chinese at all, as the *r* in rice. Most grammatical relationships in Chinese are conveyed by word order and auxiliary words. A subject and predicate often are not required in Chinese, if the context makes the meaning clear; so, "it rains" can be stated in Cantonese as "drop rain."

Some of the methods suggested for the teaching of reading in bilingual classes are reminiscent of the very careful building of basic skills we encountered earlier in teaching the handicapped. Thus, a great deal of attention is paid in some texts to the development of auditory discrimination. The teacher begins with such activities as having children list all the sounds they hear on their way home or on the playground; or children may be asked to close their eyes, make sounds by dropping a coin, or closing and opening a scissors, and guess the object used. They might play games that depend on attentive listening, such as "Simon Says." Later, pupils can be encouraged to make individual booklets with picture of words having specific sounds they need to practice.

NOTES

[1] Richard Greene, *Forgotten Children* (San Rafael, Cal.: Leswing Press, 1972), p. 35.

[2] Kathryn A. Blake, *The Mentally Retarded, An Educational Psychology* (Englewood Cliffs, N.J:. Prentice Hall, 1976), p. 65.

[3] *Ibid.*, p. 66.

7

Graduate Work

Students preparing to teach typically complete their undergraduate work and move directly into teaching positions. Most graduate programs leading to a master's degree in education require, in fact, that the candidate show evidence of some experience in the classroom as part of the admission procedure. After a year or so of teaching, many teachers enter master's programs on part-time schedules, teaching during the day and attending classes in the late afternoon and early evening.

It is possible for a person graduating from college with a liberal arts degree and no education course credits to decide, at that point or later, to fulfill the requirements for a teaching certificate by entering a graduate education program. There are several ways of doing so, such as enrolling in a special master's program created just for such students, or in a regular master's program that requires the student to complete some of the undergraduate course sequence in addition to the graduate program itself. The first of these options is the easier alternative, of course, but the special master's programs are not as available as they were a generation ago.

A number of strong trends in the profession encourage teachers to enter advanced work. Some state departments of education have been moving toward requiring a master's degree, or thirty credits of graduate work, at least, for a permanent teaching license, though a provisional license is universally granted on the basis of undergraduate work alone. (For variations among the states, see the relevant table of license requirements in the Appendix.) In addition to, or instead of, that requirement, many states offer salary increments for specified numbers of graduate credits earned. Furthermore, some professional specializations require one form of graduate work or another: most of them require at least a master's degree, and some ask for a sixty-credit certificate or the degree of Doctor of Education (Ed.D).

The following brief survey of the most common patterns of master's work in education represents some very real future choices for you, if you are seriously considering the undergraduate major. The programs described, though not of immediate interest, are part of your not too distant future.

The Early Childhood/Elementary Master's

This is usually the least demanding of the graduate programs, as well as being a state requirement most often satisfied by a specific number of credits rather than a degree. The distinction has some real meaning, since some colleges set special requirements, such as a comprehensive examination and/or a thesis, for the granting of a degree, and insist on certain required courses as well.

The elementary teaching degree is usually the M.S. (Master of Science), and may be satisfied by taking a typical thirty credits in course work (about ten or eleven courses) and fulfilling whatever special degree requirements there may be. Most students can complete this kind of program in four or five semesters, taking six to eight credits a semester; those willing to sacrifice a summer or two can shorten the period. Teachers who are settling down to careers in the elementary school or in early childhood education usually find the graduate degree flexible and not very demanding. Though they may be encouraged to take some academic work in one of the major curriculum fields they teach, most of their work is usually in professional courses, often in a workshop format focused on the activities and problems of the student participants.

As the work of elementary teachers becomes more specialized, however, the master's in elementary education tends to develop special emphases, leading to a much more structured curriculum for the graduate student. College programs taking this approach usually require a core of foundation work (nine to twelve credits), plus another nine to twelve credits in the specialization. Such requirements, it is easy to see, may well use up all but a few of the thirty master's credits, leaving the students with few choices of their own. The foundational core includes advanced work in educational psychology, an examination in depth of one of the social foundations, such as the anthropological study of schools, and one or more workshops in elementary or early childhood curriculum and teaching methods. The specialized concentration might extend and deepen one of the fields taken as an undergraduate, or offer students entry into a special field new to them. Some examples:

> Preschool settings
> Bilingual teaching
> Concentration on the deaf, or mentally retarded, etc.
> Working with the handicapped
> The plastic arts
> Music
> Remedial reading
> Mathematics and science

The Secondary Master's

In contrast to the elementary master's program, the concentration in master's work for teachers at the secondary level remains within the subject field itself: social studies, language, literature, science, etc. Somewhat fewer credits are generally required in professional courses for these students, and the credits remaining, often as many as twenty-one out of the thirty, are taken in the subject-matter field or in courses related to it. Students at this level are often urged to use the academic courses in the master's program to diversify their knowledge and skills. Thus, it is useful for science teachers with training in chemistry to take some substantial work on physics, or for former history majors now teaching social studies to develop a groundwork in economics or sociology.

There are several important educational fields for which students can prepare only at the master's level. Although these positions do not include teaching among their responsibilities, teacher preparation and some experience in the classroom are important as prerequisites to entry. In recent years a number of new support positions have been developed—school social worker, speech or hearing correction teacher, librarian, and audio/visual specialist, for example—whose training takes place outside of schools and departments of education. These fields will not be described here, although students considering an education major should be aware of the fact that they exist. We will focus, instead, on the two most important of the educational support fields, pupil personnel services, and school administration. A comprehensive survey may be found in such books as John Green's, *Fields of Teaching and Educational Services.*

Personnel Services

The enormous enterprise that is the U.S. public school system, serving fifty million children of very diverse backgrounds, talents, and needs, tries to take this diversity into account as much as possible. Though teachers can do a great deal to help their pupils negotiate the system successfully, and make decisions about their future as adults after they leave school, they are too busy, with their primary task of helping children learn, to take on very much of the task of counseling and guidance. That task is primarily the concern of a special staff within the school district, under the direction of a director of pupil personnel services.

The size of the staff depends on the number of pupils in the district, and on the resources of the community, but all school systems offer some form of service. In very small districts the special education teachers for handicapped children may be included under this administrative umbrella, but the upsurge of federal interest in the handicapped has in most places resulted in the development of a separate department of special education.

The pupil personnel program itself usually includes guidance counselors, school psychologists, pupil attendance workers (formerly known as "truant officers!") and school social workers. Little in the way of academic preparation is required for the attendance workers, and school social workers graduate from regular social work programs. The first two positions—guidance counselor and psychologist—listed are key specialties of education graduate programs.

Guidance Counselor. The school guidance program has traditionally emphasized vocational counseling, but more recently the task of the guidance counselor has expanded to a more comprehensive role including personal counseling, group guidance activities, orientation of pupils to services available in the school, vocational and higher education guidance, and job placement and follow-up. Guidance has also developed some specializations of its own, vocational rehabilitation counseling, for example, which helps those with physical, emotional, or mental handicaps find productive work.

Certification requirements for guidance counselors in most states include not only teaching but often nonschool work experience, such as work with children in a mental health setting. Most of the graduate programs that train counselors demand a strong core of course work in psychology and the behavioral sciences, followed by a sequence of professional courses in counseling and psychological and vocational testing. A practicum—supervised field practice in a school or other setting—is generally included, not only to give students necessary practical experience, but as a final test of ability.

School Psychologist. Whereas the guidance counselor tries to work with as many of the school's pupils as possible, the school psychologist concentrates on the 10 percent or so who most need psychological services; the emotionally maladjusted, the handicapped, and the gifted. Psychologists are responsible for operating the group testing program (including the administration of IQ tests if the school gives them), doing case studies of individual children about whom the school must make a diagnosis or a special curriculum assignment, providing formal and informal in-service training in psychological problems for the school's teachers, and developing research projects or helping teachers who wish to write case studies of children requiring special help.

The bulk of a school psychologist's time is spent helping pupils referred to him or her by teachers who feel that they cannot deal with the problem of a particular child, and in testing and diagnosis of children in need of special treatment.

The curriculum for future guidance counselors is the less demanding of the two fields. The program begins with an introductory course that reviews various aspects of the guidance role, then proceeds to specialized courses that develop the necessary skills of the counselor. The following topics are representative of those that students will encounter:

1. A consideration of the relation of the guidance role to the general functions of the school, usually with some attention given to the philosophical issues; some educators believe, for instance, that the personal and emotional growth of the child should be the central concern of the school, whereas others think that intellectual learning is much more important.

2. A description of pupil personnel services in the schools, and how they are organized and administered. This may include a review of the qualifications required to fill the various positions included in these services, and the overlapping roles played by those who occupy the positions.

3. A detailed discussion of pupil testing methods, and how and where the results of the testing program are reported. These include academic aptitude tests, achievement instruments, surveys of interests and attitudes, and personality inventories.

4. Organizing systems of information about pupils, developing and maintaining cumulative record forms, etc.

5. The influence of guidance on the development of curriculum, and on pupils' response to the classroom learning situation; the importance of cooperation between guidance counselor and teacher, with an emphasis on methods of working with teachers.

6. Basic counseling procedures, how to conduct counseling interviews, and the relation of counseling to psychotherapy; helping children plan for careers, and the organization and communication of occupational information.

111

Preparation for a school psychologist position is both longer and more academically demanding. Students who wish to consider becoming school psychologists should major in either education or psychology at the undergraduate level; if the former is chosen, psychology should be selected as a minor. Full certification as a school psychologist, it should be realized, involves taking a long, hard road, and the academically faint-hearted should think twice before starting. Depending on the particular state in which students plan to work, the position may require a doctorate or three years of work in psychology. A provisional license may require somewhat less academic preparation, but this type of license assumes supervision, and does not allow for tenure.

Here is an example of a set of recommendations for combined undergraduate and graduate work for the position of school psychologist:

> 24 credits in psychological foundations of education
> 24 credits in psychological methods and testing techniques
> 18 credits in other educational foundations and in school curriculum and organization
> Over 500 hours of supervised field experience over the course of an academic year

School Administration

Even at the elementary school level the administrative staff of schools has diversified and mushroomed just in the last twenty years. In addition to a principal, a school of any size will have an assistant principal and a curriculum coordinator. In the high school, in addition to one or two assistant principals with specialized duties, several administrators will be assigned to pupil personnel services, and each major department will have a supervisor. All this is apart from a number of persons who may be directly responsible for such support services as business management, food service, etc. In a fairly large district an even greater number of administrative positions may be found at central headquarters, where the school superintendent in charge has increasingly complex matters to deal with.

Those students who are thinking a long way ahead to what division of the educational field they might like to specialize in may find it useful to realize that there are several important differences among program offerings in the field. The most important distinction is probably the one that divides those graduate programs stressing *human relations* as the most important areas of skill for the school administrator, from the programs emphasizing *managerial skills*. This difference is only partly due to the variety of administrative positions; the elementary school principal, for example, does work more closely with teachers and has more need for human relations skills than the high school principal. But, in addition, the field of administration itself tends to disagree about which of these approaches is the most important.

The texts and materials for study in the field tend to carry one or another of these emphases. The human relations-based text, for example, is likely to include a good deal on the following topics of organization for instruction:

Detailed consideration of the various school organization plans, including discussion of the need to decentralize authority, and study of methods for organizing teacher resources, team teaching, etc.

The principal's role in improving the motivation of pupils, and in helping students develop their own pupil-planned activities, such as clubs, newspapers, etc.

Evaluating the instructional program; defining goals and developing a philosophy of education for the school, and helping teachers in defining their own evaluation responsibilities.

Improving instruction through supervision, both the kind that is exercised through other members of the administrative staff and those supervisory activities the principal performs.

Building staff morale, and involving the entire staff in the development of policies and rules.

Dealing with "problem pupils," including the gifted, who need special enrichment, and those who are handicapped or maladjusted.

Key words and phrases of the human relations approach to administration have deliberately been used above: motivation, participation, morale, helping, concern for pupil activities, etc. Although a text taking the alternative approach, emphasizing managerial skills, may deal with many of the same issues, the language and definition of the principals' activities are very different: patterns of school organization, management of the staff, the school plant as an environment for learning, maintenance and operation of the school, administration of supplies and equipment, management of the school cafeteria, public relations and school administration, staff growth through in-service education, etc. These headings reflect a more recent, and much "cooler" view of school administration. University programs are so varied that students, fortunately, may select the emphasis they themselves prefer.

The most common, as well as one of the most important school administrative positions is the principalship, and it is on preparing for that role that this brief review of specific course work focuses. Other school and district positions, such as assistant principal, dean of students, or responsibility for personnel or for community and public relations, usually require training that is very similar to parts of the course work included in the preparation for principals. Although only twenty years ago the master's degree was the usual educational credential of the principal, two full years of graduate work are now commonly required for the position, and in the larger cities there is a steady trend toward the view that the doctorate (an Ed.D. rather than a Ph.D.) is also desirable. A program of preparation for the principalship increasingly includes the following elements:

> Philosophy, psychology, and sociology of education
>
> Supervision, including methods involved in selecting, training, and evaluating teachers
>
> Human behavior, particularly the psychology of motivation and the relation of personality to work
>
> Group processes, including techniques for involving people in planning and problem solving, and group influences on the level of productive work by small groups
>
> Curriculum development: the establishment of educa-

tional goals that will meet the requirements of both community and the professional staff

Communication skills: oral and written reports, writing press releases and bulletins, making speeches to community groups

Community relations: understanding of community structure and the network of agencies affecting the school's work, and techniques for working with them

School law and finance, including the nuts and bolts of labor relations as well as an understanding of the process of working with governmental agencies

It is clear from these very demanding training objectives why, until recently, most of those with sufficient incentive to take on the challenge of school administration training were men, and why, consequently, so many principals were men. This has changed considerably, and the sex distribution is becoming much more equal.

For those who are interested in working with people and who get a great deal of satisfaction out of making things go, preparatory work for the administrative role can be fascinating in itself. One such graduate program, for example, includes the following elements: fifteen credits in foundation work, the first objective in the list above; nine credits in an "admissions core" devoted first, to taking a number of diagnostic tests, including face-to-face interviews, plus a comprehensive study of a community, its history and geography, economic life, politics and power structures, formal and informal organizations, and school systems and other educational agencies; eighteen to twenty-one credits in advanced studies, involving a selection of courses taught mostly by professors in other colleges or departments of the university, studies that might include economics, speech, business management, and public administration; six to nine credits of specialized work relating to the specific position aimed for: elementary principal, high school principal, business manager, director of curriculum, etc.; nine credits of supervised field experience, either one full-time semester, or part-time for a year.

Administration programs have also been moving increasingly away from the formal class/lecture method to a variety of interesting and much more personally involving learning techniques: case studies, role-playing, simulation games, and other activities that students may not be familiar with. The case study has been very much a part of administrative training for many years; it presents students with a detailed description of a situation that must be dealt with, and provides an opportunity to discuss the usefulness of various solutions proposed by class members. Gaming is a more recent development; developed to a high art in both military and industrial training, it involves students in an elaborate recreation of reality, with different participants playing a variety of roles in the situation, trying to solve problems as though in real life. "In-basket exercises," a variation of the simulation technique, provide individual participants with a stack of letters, memoranda, telephone messages, etc., of the kind that a school administrator might find in his in-basket some morning, and require students to go through the material and indicate what action is to be taken for each communication.

Beyond the Master's Degree

The Ed.D. is the most commonly encountered doctorate in education, with the Ph.D. in Education (the research degree) becoming comparatively rare. Some of the top administrative posts, such as that of superintendent (in the largest cities) will probably require the Ed.D. in the near future, and many of those in charge of curriculum or evaluation divisions in the larger school systems now already have the degree.

An Ed.D. program usually requires sixty credits of graduate work beyond the master's, and the successful completion of a doctoral project that makes a significant original contribution to education, such as the design and testing of a new curriculum for a special target group of students.

The greatest concentration of doctorate holders is on university faculties, among those who teach the courses we have been describing, who conduct the research on which the textbooks are based, and who write those textbooks. The route to college teaching in education is somewhat different from the one that leads to positions on liberal-arts faculties. Most professors of education begin as regular teachers or administrators in a school system. Increasing school experience and graduate work in education (often including a specialized certificate program beyond the master's degree) help to move them into a few courses a year as adjunct faculty in a college. Then, when positions open, they become full-time faculty members. Though other, more academic, paths exist, this is the most common one.

8

Teaching as a Career

More students prepare for careers in teaching than actually enter the profession. Many more enter the field than stay in it for more than a few years. Chapter 1 suggested that one of the reasons for the first of these facts is that for many years teaching was considered, particularly for young women, something to "fall back on" in a jobless emergency. But the primary reasons for the turnover are more complicated; early teacher dropout is due, in part, simply to the decision of young married couples to start having families of their own; it can also be partly explained by the idealistic expectations that some young and inexperienced teachers carry with them into the real world of the classroom.

This chapter and the next one explore these and other "real" issues. If you have concluded by this point that preparing for a teaching career sounds like an interesting way of spending part of the college years, you will find it profitable to make this brief exploration of the realities of the job market and the problems and rewards of school life.

Desirable Qualities

Each profession demands special qualities of those who practice it—certain physical and mental abilities, and a willingness to bear the particular strains imposed. Each profession also develops over the years at least a rough idea of what kind of person is happiest and does best in the professional role. Here are some of the qualities that commonly turn up on lists of good teacher characteristics, a list against which readers might wish to measure themselves:

leadership ability: as evidenced by activity in student groups, by whether fellow students turn to you for advice and help, a willingness to listen to what others have to say, success at getting others to follow suggestions.

physical fitness: although physically handicapped persons are being encouraged to enter teaching, teaching usually requires more vitality than many people realize (and also requires the ability to remain even-tempered when tired).

academic ability: as evidenced by a better-than-average school record, an ability to concentrate, success at expressing ideas before groups and in class, a readiness to explore topics that interest you beyond the effort required to complete an assignment, a desire to excel.

emotional stability: as evidenced by a good deal of patience and tolerance of others, a sense of humor and a willingness to laugh at oneself, an ability to be critical of one's own performance and take criticism from others.

interest in helping others: as evidenced by an interest in other people's problems, a general liking for people, especially children.

What Administrators Look For

Many of the foregoing qualities are very difficult to make judgments about in the often brief interviews that principals or central office administrators have with young graduates looking for their first positions. A survey of over one hundred junior and senior high school principals in the midwest[1] revealed that they look for much more obvious things: neat physical appearance, a favorable letter of recommendation from the applicant's cooperating teacher, and clearly stated professional goals. Some of the other things principals in the survey agreed were important included:

119

Emotional balance	94% agreed was important
Possession of a "sound educational philosophy"	94%
Ability to provide for individual differences	90%
A strong desire to work	84%
Youth (between 20 and 25)	83%
Good command of English	70%
Confidence and enthusiasm	70%
Voice quality	70%

Although teacher training will be sure to provide many ideas for how to take account of individual differences in the classroom, the second item in the list presents a tricky problem for any professional. Since there is so much argument about philosophies of education, and since everyone considers his or her own philosophy to be the sound one, what is a candidate to do? The best answer is probably to express one's honest views undogmatically.

As teaching jobs have become less plentiful, some school districts are setting up even more elaborate teacher selection procedures. For example, a Pennsylvania district, after having all candidates interviewed by the district personnel director, selects the four to six best qualified and invites them back for an interview with the principal and a committee of teachers from the school that has the vacancy. Each member of the committee rates the individual candidates on: initiative, compatibility, knowledge, and personality. The candidates complete a teacher attitude measure that scores them for their leaning toward either the teacher-centered or the student-centered approach to learning. Each candidate also teaches a ten-minute videotaped mini-lesson to a small group of students. The committee analyzes all the material, then takes a vote on the candidates; the one with the most votes is generally recommended to the board of education for hiring.

Supply and Demand

In the half-century between 1920 and 1970 the number of teachers at both elementary and secondary levels increased dramatically, from about seven hundred thousand to well over two million. Furthermore, in the first decade of that period, secondary teachers represented only one out of every seven teachers, but by the end of the 1960s there were about as many teachers in secondary schools as in elementary schools. In the latest part of that span of years, from about 1950 on, the rise in the number of teachers was especially noticeable as the baby crop that followed World War II began to swell school enrollments.

Those same babies began to move out of the public schools in the late 1960s, and what had been a chronic teacher short-age was reversed in the early 1970s. The number of teachers did not itself decline; what happened was that the demand for new teachers, instead of rising as it had for decades, leveled off. And, although the supply of teachers also dropped, as fewer college students enrolled in teacher preparation courses, the number of students graduating with teacher credentials con-tinued to be somewhat higher than the positions available.

In the not-very-distant future, happily, the supply and demand forces that create available teaching positions will be much more favorable for those entering the profession. By 1985 the modestly rising birth rate of the late 1970s will result in more children entering the elementary school, thus increasing the demand for teachers. At the same time, the number of students graduating from college prepared to look for teaching positions will *decrease*, because students of that age will have been born from 1963 on, when the birth rate began to decline.

In the immediate period, before these shifts occur, students planning for their own future and genuinely interested in a teaching career should not be overly pessimistic, for several reasons at least. First, though the job market is nothing like the former one, in which beginning teachers could walk into a position, and often pick and choose among them, a longer job search does not mean that there is not a teaching position avail-able. Second, the national picture often obscures local needs; in 1978 the largest city in the country was so desperately in need of secondary school teachers that officials induced local universities to operate a crash summer program to produce them. Third, even without another rise in births during the 1980s (not very likely), changes in educational policy will produce a rising demand for specialized teachers, such as those noted in Chapter 6. For example, the supply of beginning teachers in the area of special education has increased since 1973, as that of most others declined. And, although federal agencies are pressing very hard for racially integrated faculties in the schools, the number of black and Hispanic students of education has seldom been large enough to maintain even the present proportion of those groups in the national teacher supply.

The demand for specialized teachers changes from year to year, and students interested in a particular area should check sources of information on the current labor market. In the mid-1970s, for example, although there were more teacher education graduates in such general fields as social studies and language arts than there were jobs available, there were more jobs than graduates in science and mathematics, elementary physical education, and industrial and technical trades.

Private Schools

Although teacher preparation institutions themselves do not distinguish between public and private schools in their training, a person considering a career in education should be aware that private schools do offer a somewhat different career path. About 15 percent of U.S. children attend parochial schools, private boarding and day schools, preparatory schools, and military academies, and there are perhaps a quarter of a million teaching positions in these schools.

Almost all of them charge tuition fees—rather modest ones in the case of the religion-based schools—and they can set their own standards of admission, a very important consideration for some teachers who wish to work with selected pupil groups, such as the gifted. Selectivity also results in a much more homogeneous pupil population than one can usually find in public schools, a condition that many teachers find makes their work much easier.

From a career point of view, teaching in private schools has both advantages and disadvantages. Administrators are much freer to hire teachers without the interference of bureaucratic restrictions, and they are free to adjust salaries to fit individual needs or merits. Salary schedules, on the other hand, are usually lower than in most public school systems, job security is almost nonexistent, and fringe benefits (sick leave, holidays, health insurance, etc.) are generally less substantial. For many teachers who seek positions in private schools by choice, however, the advantages easily outweigh these disadvantages.

Career Patterns

About a third of the children in the United States go to school in rural or small-town districts, where teachers' careers are fairly predictable, and where they usually stay within a single district. The rest of the country's teachers are employed within metropolitan areas, in cities or the suburbs around them. For many years, teachers have often transferred in mid-career from poor and working-class districts in the cities to the suburban schools as they acquire experience and are able to get more "desirable" positions.

Along with this general movement from city to suburb (much the same kind of shift that has taken place in the city-rural population as a whole), a noticeable aspect of the teacher career has been its high dropout rate. To take St. Louis as an example: of the beginning teachers in 1968, only six out of ten were still teaching a year later, only four out of ten were still in the system three years later, and after six years, less than one of four were still teaching.[2] Some of these teachers may have moved to other systems in the state or outside it, some may have switched from full-time teaching to part-time, sporadic teaching, butt he majority probably just dropped out of the profession altogether. The dropout rate is highest for young and inexperienced teachers, and particularly for women.

Although these trends have persisted in more recent years, the decline in the job market discussed earlier has modified them considerably, because:

1. Teachers are still moving from the central city to the fringes of metropolitan areas, but the amount of such movement has been decreasing as the growth of suburban areas themselves has leveled off.

2. Teacher dropout rates have themselves been steadily dropping, and the dropout rates are highest *not* in the central city schools, where teaching is considered to be more challenging, but in the outer, suburban schools.

3. Schools in every ring of the metropolitan area, from the central city to the furthest suburb, have been carrying over almost 90 percent of the staffs they had the year before, a much higher percentage than before the change in the job market. As a result, the percentage of experienced teachers has been rising.

4. The number of people in administrative, non-teaching, positions as well as their proportion to the total staff, has been increasing steadily almost everywhere, whether pupil enrollment has increased or declined.

Salaries

By the mid-1970s teacher salaries nationwide averaged $12,524, about $5,000 more a year than the average in the mid-1960s. Although this is an increase of about 40 percent in dollar amounts, in actual purchasing power, with price inflation taken into account, the increase was only 1 percent.[3]

National averages can obscure a good deal of variation in different parts of the country, however. Another somewhat misleading result of averaging is to obscure the fact that about half the teachers in each state are earning more than the average figure; because most states provide automatic salary increases with experience, many of the teachers below the state average are the youngest, with the least experience. So, for example, the median teacher salary for New York state was $15,950 in 1975–76, but with a reasonable number of years in the system and extra college credits, many New York City teachers were earning over $20,000 a year, although the entry salary for beginning teachers was about $10,000. Many teachers, of course, can and do supplement their incomes by working during the summer months as teachers, summer camp staff, or in special federal programs such as Head Start.

It is difficult, of course, to predict what will happen in the future, but four of the forces that act either to increase or decrease teacher salaries are briefly noted below:

1. Much of what happened to the purchasing power of the teacher salary in the ten-year period described above was due to a severe inflation that wiped out substantial dollar gains. A lower rate of inflation in the 1980s will help preserve gains of all salaried workers; teachers are by no means the only victims of the inflationary spiral.

2. A growing force that will, in the future, tend to retard teacher salary gains is the resistance of local taxpayers to the rising costs of local government. In almost all school districts a major part of school budgets is covered by property taxes, against which there has been a rising clamor of protest. School budgets also are often the only local government cost for which taxpayers vote specifically; in recent years, consequently, taxpayers across the country have turned down about as many school budgets as they have approved.

3. On the other hand, the organization of teacher unions and their growing militancy has operated to improve salaries, and, where salary gains have been somewhat held back by other forces, teacher unions often manage to improve other fringe benefits such as family health insurance and extra pay for extracurricular activities.

4. There is a very sizeable movement in many states to equalize the amounts that the school districts in the state spend on education. One way of doing that is to shift a larger share of school costs from local district taxes to the state tax system. As this movement grows, some of the resistance to school taxes at the local level will be neutralized.

Rewards of the Profession

Most of the career issues we have dealt with so far apply equally to elementary and secondary teachers, though some districts still have separate salary schedules for the two levels, a fact that beginning teachers should keep in mind in their preliminary job search. But the rewards that teachers get from their careers consist of much more than their salaries and fringe benefits; one of the major advantages that professions have over other vocations, indeed, is that they provide nonmaterial as well as material rewards. And it is in this area of psychological and social payoffs that teaching levels vary.

Within the broad range of teaching levels, secondary school teaching falls between college instruction and the elementary grades, as the first chapter made clear. The concentration on subject matter and research in the university attracts, for the most part, people who enjoy those activities. At the secondary level, junior and senior high school teachers get some of the reward that comes from mastering knowledge; in addition, they work a good deal with one another in subject-matter departments, and therefore can achieve satisfaction from the camaraderie as well as the approval and respect of their colleagues.

The way in which the elementary school is organized, however, results in a very different system of personal rewards for teachers, which appears strikingly in a survey of Florida teachers.[4] They were asked about the types of rewards that are important for them in three different aspects of the teaching career. Here is how they responded:

Rewards from teaching activity itself:

Chance to study, read, and plan for classes	3.4%
Discipline and classroom management	1.0
Knowing that I have "reached" students and they have learned	86.6
Chance to associate with children or young people	7.6
Chance to associate with other teachers	1.0
No satisfaction from these	.3

Rewards from being a member of the profession:

Security of income and position	22.9
Time (esp. summers) for travel, etc.	23.2
Freedom from competition, rivalry	5.2
Appropriateness for people like me	34.4
No satisfaction from these	14.4

Rewards external to teaching:

Salary	15.5
Respect from others	37.8
Chance to use influence	34.0
No satisfaction from these	12.6

When the teachers were asked which of these three different types of reward is more important compared to the others, the result was very enlightening:

Teaching itself	77.8%
Professional membership	11.1
External to teaching	11.0

Elementary teachers, it is clear, get their reward overwhelmingly from the teaching activity itself, and within that activity, from seeing children learn. This very substantial agreement is probably due to the self-contained classroom of the elementary school. Because teachers spend almost the entire day in the same room with the same group of children, they get the chance to speak to colleagues only during coffee breaks and sometimes during lunch. If the school does not employ some form of team teaching, neither do they get a chance to see each other teach. This concentration of time and energy within the classroom makes it inevitably the focus for their sense of accomplishment. When the Florida teachers were asked how they would use a gift of ten or more hours per week, which would have to be used in some form of work, almost all of them mentioned some teaching activity, or counseling of pupils, instead of out-of-classroom activities like curriculum planning, work with parents, etc.

Professional Growth

One of the major trends in almost all service professions— medicine and nursing, social work, therapy, etc.—is the requirement of continuing education that will keep the professional up to date on new knowledge and skills in the field. The increasingly common demand that teachers take at least thirty additional graduate credits beyond the bachelor degree is part of that trend, but by no means completely satisfies it. Those who choose teaching as a career may expect to be involved in periodic in-service training, apart from the accreditation requirements of formal university work.

Most teachers welcome in-service training conducted within

the system itself, especially if it focuses clearly on the specific teaching problems they encounter daily, because they seldom feel that their college sequence did a very complete job of preparation. To demonstrate how strong those feelings can be, and the areas of preparation in which beginning teachers feel inadequately supported by their college training, here are some of the responses from a survey of secondary teachers six months after graduation:[5]

Teaching Skill	% regarding it as important or very important	% regarding their training as effective or very effective
Classroom control techniques	96%	20%
Using audio-visual media	68	56
Discussing controversial issues	59	42
Giving directions to pupils	93	71
Leading discussions	86	61
Lesson planning	72	43
Applying learning psychology	65	29
Individualizing instruction	75	44
Constructing tests	75	48
Using performance objectives	45	60
Identifying curriculum trends	49	32
Using different instructional modes	83	51
Maintaining effective teacher-student relationships	94	28

Although some of these estimates of the effectiveness of training reflect the great pressures involved in the first year of teaching and to some extent the difficulty of learning certain skills outside the real situation of the classroom, they also indicate the areas of greatest need for support for beginning teachers. Some school systems provide supervisors to give such help in the first few years; others add a staff development program that operates after school or in a concentrated series of seminars in the summer.

Few systems run as complete a staff development program as does Hartford, Connecticut for a group of four schools in a black and Hispanic area of the city (Project Train). A note of the project activities will convey some idea of the possibilities. During one academic year a variety of separate courses were offered, including multicultural approaches to education, instructional management, prescriptive-diagnostic techniques for teaching reading, and children's literature for inner-city children. During the summer, intensive institutes based on the clinical experience of the participants were held on such topics as exceptional children, mathematics and metric education, and words-in-color approach to teaching reading. The project then began a series of seminars for small groups of teachers who worked together in teams, focusing on helping them with specific classroom problems, and also conducted a lecture series for full staff on early-dismissal days.

The Hartford project has put into practice a number of in-service training principles that are becoming increasingly accepted in the training of teachers: providing on-site instruction and seminar discussion; offering a great range of situations, from lecture to peer teaching; giving attention to staff needs and problems focusing on actual competence rather than formal credentials; establishing contacts with the community and with state agencies.

Professional Organizations

Most teachers find it useful to belong to at least one major organization devoted to their interests, and usually join several: at least one that helps keep them abreast of their major skill area, and another focused on their broader professional and vocational concerns. The two major organizations now in the field, the National Education Association (NEA), and the American Federation of Teachers (AFT) are among the second type of broad range associations, with the NEA attempting to fulfill both functions.

The National Education Association

The NEA is the oldest organization for teachers in the country, having started in the middle of the last century. Its membership has risen from a few thousand around the turn of the century, to 1.8 million today; in the early 1900s it was given a special national charter by Congress.

The all-embracing interests of the organization are reflected in statements of goals and objectives that in one way or another reach every possible educational concern. The major current goals are listed below, with a few illustrative objectives under each:

Human and civil rights in education: Support for teachers' rights of all sorts, and for the rights of minorities and women; training of teachers for special demands of school desegregation, etc.

Leadership in solving social problems: with special emphasis on the education of migrant children and the reduction of violence in the schools.

Expansion: a membership goal of 1.9 million; provisions of leadership training for local and state organizations; coordination of services, etc.

Professional excellence: conduct of research into teaching effectiveness; in-service training for teachers, etc.

Economic and professional security: lobbying on collective bargaining legislation; support of collective bargaining efforts by local affiliates; enforcement of teacher contract provisions, etc.

Significant legislative support for public education: lobbying for increased federal aid; election of pro-education candidates to local and federal office, etc.

The NEA is, in fact, an enormous umbrella covering not only its own departments which publish and distribute a vast amount of helpful material (see Chapter 11 for the address of its Publications Division), but a number of special teacher organizations that affiliate with it, such as the Association for Supervision and Curriculum Development, and also many of the groups representing separate academic disciplines. So a social studies teacher who joins the professional social studies teaching organization usually also becomes automatically a member of the NEA, with which the organization is affiliated.

The American Federation of Teachers

This union organization was founded in 1918 as an affiliate of the AFL, which later merged with the CIO to become the present national federation of labor unions. The 1960s was its greatest period of expansion, as it grew from 60,000 to 600,000 members. The union includes not only elementary and secondary teachers, but 100,000 college professors and a growing number of paraprofessionals.

AFT objectives appropriately stress the bargaining rights of teachers, but also include striving for teachers' rights, improved standards of teaching through in-service training, the improvement of education generally, and child welfare.

The two organizations, in many ways, have come to resemble each other in purpose over the years. The NEA once insisted that teachers should not strike, but slowly came to use the strike weapon itself as the AFT showed how successful it could be. The AFT has, on the other hand, broadened its view of the union role to include many of the purely professional concerns that were once the exclusive preserve of the NEA. The possibility of merger into one larger organization has long been discussed, and the negotiations are resumed every few years or so, only to be broken off.

The major strength of the AFT is based in the city school systems; that of the NEA is still based on state affiliates, which are often controlled by rural and small-town teachers and administrators. Although major differences in philosophy and organization have so far kept the two organizations separate, they are usually on the same side of most education policy arguments, and many teachers find it useful to belong to both.

NOTES

[1] Bobby R. Johnson, "What Administrators Look For in Teacher Interviews," *Phi Delta Kappan*, November 1976, pp. 283–84.
[2] Barry D. Anderson and Jonathan Mark, "Teacher Mobility and Productivity in a Metropolitan Area, A Seven Year Case Study," *Urban Education* 12 (April 1977), 15–35.

[3] Richard A. Musemeche and Sam Adams, "The Rise and Fall of Teachers' Salaries: A Nine-Region Survey," *Phi Delta Kappan*, February 1977, pp. 479–81.

[4] Dan C. Lortie, "The Balance of Control and Autonomy in Elementary School," Amitai Etzioni, ed., *The Semi Professions and Their Organization* (New York: Free Press, 1969), p. 32.

[5] R. Stephen Rosser and Jon J. Denton, "Assessing Recent Teacher Education Graduates Using a Two-Scaled Instrument," *Education*, Vol. 98, No. 1, pp. 102–103.

9
Life in School

A Typical Day

It would clearly be difficult to give a very complete picture of what teaching in a school is like, considering the vast variety of schools and the very different individual needs of those who seek to teach in them. This chapter, therefore, takes only a few soundings into some of the more important aspects of school life. We begin with the broad picture—a typical day in a second grade classroom.[1]

The children sit in five rows of six seats each, in a bright and cheerful room. Supplies, games, and books are arranged on a series of low shelves that run around the room, and other books are displayed more prominently on top of the shelves. The alphabet, in large letters, runs along the top of the blackboards in the front of the room, there are house plants sitting on the teacher's desk, and on the walls, bulletin boards displaying children's drawings and papers. Also displayed is a chart listing the classroom management duties assigned to various children: duster, messenger, morning leader, in charge of pencils, etc.

Some children come by buses on different schedules, and the room gradually fills from 8:30 to 9:00. It is Monday, so the teacher, an attractive, smiling woman, must collect snack and lunch money. Also this morning she collects permission slips from parents, one set for some immunization shots, another for a trip to a fire station to be taken later in the week. It takes her half an hour to complete her recording of money collected and permissions received; during that time the children are instructed to copy the "morning news" written on the board, and, quiet and orderly, they do so.

As soon as the pupils finish the task, they begin to get restless. The teacher tells them to recopy the news—"it will be good practice"—but some start talking and soon, despite some admonition from the teacher, they get noisier. But the teacher ultimately finishes her task, sends the records off to the office, and the class settles down.

"Now it's share time," says the teacher, and the morning leader, Phyllis, comes to the front to manage the activity. Joyce has brought a book to share, and is encouraged to read it to the class. The children respond with delight, while the teacher watches, smiling. At the end, she compliments both girls and the class as well for their participation.

From 10:00 to 12:30 the children engage in a variety of reading and arithmetic lessons—with a short break for recess at 10:30. The class has been divided into three groups by reading ability. The Bluebirds, in the back of the room, are given a word task (to copy sentences with rhyming words and underline each pair), while the Robins and the Larks have board work on a new type of arithmetic. There are ten problems on the blackboard, and the children vie with one another to give the answers to them. Then all the children work individually on reading exercises, while the teacher either works at her desk or walks up and down the aisles looking at their papers as they work.

Then it is recess time, and the children get their coats and leave the building. The teacher forms two teams and they play a running game; later, after a few minutes of free play, everyone is back in the classroom, by 10:45. There is great disorder while coats are hung up and milk is passed around; before all the children have finished their milk about fifteen minutes have passed. The teacher puts up a sign with "Happy Birthday, Teresa" on it, to a chorus of "Happy Birthday" from the children. One of the bottles of milk falls and breaks, and a janitor comes to remove the broken glass.

Then the groups go back to their reading lessons, the teacher working with each group individually for a time, mainly asking to hear individual recitations. All children are back in their seats by 12:15, at which point the teacher admonishes them about making noise during the reading lessons. She points out that some children have not yet finished their work, and instructs them to stay inside after lunch and finish up, while those who have finished can play outside. At 12:25 lines have been formed, and the class walks to the cafeteria.

The teacher ignores a certain amount of punching and jostling among the boys, gets the children through the food lines, and picks up her own lunch. She eats with the children, who comment to her about happenings at home, new toys, etc. Then, back to the room, where the delinquents settle down to finish their morning work while the others go outside to play. The teacher is free to spend the half-hour that remains with other teachers, in the comfortably furnished teachers' room.

Everyone is herded back and arithmetic lessons are ready to begin by 1:35; they continue to 2:00. One of the children goes to the bathroom and is heard to be crying; he refuses to come out at the teacher's request—he has wet his pants. He finally emerges after the children leave the room for recess, and is accompanied by the teacher to the office for some dry clothes while the janitor is called to clean up.

The teacher's absence from the playground induces some wild play among the children, and when they come back in at 2:15 she tells them to rest with their heads on the desk. She foregoes lessons, and reads a story to the class instead. Then it is time to put things away and get ready to leave. The teacher reminds them of the spelling test the next day, while the class mills about getting their things together in the last fifteen minutes of the day. The teacher works at her desk on records, interrupted by a stream of questions from children and by bus departure announcements over the loudspeaker. The children who walk home are dismissed at 3:00.

The teacher straightens the room, sharpens a batch of pencils, and stacks the papers that must be corrected later. She works on her lesson plan for the following day, and prepares some special materials she will need. It is almost 4:00 by the time she is ready to leave.

Although representative in a number of ways, this day in the life of a teacher tells only a small part of the general story. (It certainly explains why beginning teachers complain of fatigue by the time they get home each day.) One would find a somewhat different use of time in a junior or senior high school classroom, where the teacher meets a different group of students every hour or so, and where the occasional role of "mother" in relation to children shifts to one of "guide."

Even within the instructional role itself, different teachers and teachers at different levels will emphasize one aspect rather than another. Some experts define three different kinds of instructional activity in classrooms, each of which was described in the classroom day above: *recitation, class-task,* and *multitask.* The first involves a large group of pupils in a single task, responding to questions raised by the teacher. This activity is very frequent at both the elementary and secondary level. *Class tasks* are activities in which pupils work on tests, workbooks, or assignments, either individually or in small groups, but in which all are doing the same thing. This is also common in classrooms at all levels, though it is probably emphasized more at the lower levels. *Multitask* activities consist of small group and independent tasks, in which students work on different projects or tasks at the same time. Although this type of classroom work is found in shops and laboratories in secondary schools, it tends to be much more typical of classrooms in the elementary school.

Even in a specific school, however, individual teachers are usually free to develop the kind of task mix they feel most comfortable with. Studies in elementary schools, for example, show that teachers differ a great deal in their use of time; some teachers use recitation as little as 20 percent of the time, others as much as 50 or 60 percent. But, as our account also shows, teachers spend a good deal of time on non-instructional tasks. In a typical work week the average mix of elementary teacher activities, in a forty-eight-and-one-half-hour week, is:[2]

Class instruction, 29 hours, 30 minutes
Related out-of-class instructional activities, 11 hours, 54
    minutes

Correcting papers: 3 hrs., 54 mins.
Preparing materials: 3 hrs., 42 mins.
Planning: 2 hrs., 30 mins.
Individual help: 54 mins.
Parent contacts: 54 mins.
Miscellaneous activities
Monitorial duties: 2 hrs., 54 mins.
Records and reports: 1 hr., 54 mins.
Official meetings: 48 mins.
Other: 1 hr., 30 mins.

Secondary teachers meet with 150 different students during their day, and spend:

23.6 hours in class instruction
13.3 hours in related out-of-class activities
9 hours in miscellanous activities

Teachers and the Goals of the School

Although the second graders in our "typical day" appeared to be spending most of their learning time on reading and arithmetic, the teacher was, in fact, also concerned with their learning other things such as manners, concentration on tasks, compliance with orders by superiors, independence, concern for others, and many other goals of education. Some of these social goals are apparent even in the abbreviated version of the classroom day given here; the more complete description from which it was taken gives further details of these kinds of interaction between the teacher and the children.

The U.S. school system does indeed have a great many goals for the children with whom it spends so much time, and consequently makes a variety of demands on the teacher. A representative selection of these goals is given in Table 2; they are part of a longer list of sixty aims of schooling presented to a large number of citizens of Massachusetts, who were asked to indicate how important each one was.[3]

It should be noted that the goals are listed in order of their importance to the respondents: 80 percent of all those asked thought that the first one was "very important"; only 8 percent

137

Table 2. Educational Goals as Ranked by Different Groups

"As a result of his or her experience in the public schools, each student . . ."

Percent of Each Group Responding "very important"

RANK	GOAL	PARENTS	TEACHERS	STUDENTS
1	. . . has the self-confidence to do what he knows is right in spite of outside pressure . . .	85	81	68
2	. . . develops a high level of self-knowledge and self-respect . . .	80	78	61
3	. . . can solve problems, reason intelligently, and identify faulty thinking . . .	81	76	56
4	. . . develops good learning habits, and expects to use them for the rest of his life . . .	85	73	53
5	. . . has the work skills and work attitudes needed to get and hold a job . . .	77	75	62
7	. . . understands what he reads well enough for use in his daily life . . .	79	79	47
8	. . . understands and respects the personal dignity and contribution of every human being . . .	73	82	59
17	. . . understands the laws of the nation and is committed to obeying them . . .	64	54	41
24	. . . understands that all living things depend on each other, and that anything which threatens one life form can also threaten other life forms . . .	56	53	45
35	. . . experiences a variety of work-related activities during his school years . . .	46	42	33

41	. . . performs appropriate computational tasks successfully . . .	37	45	20
42	. . . is committed to improving our goverment, our laws, and our political system . . .	37	36	23
46	. . . participates in and enjoys many beneficial physical activities throughout his life . . .	27	24	30
47	. . . has done creative things, such as drawing, painting, acting, singing, or playing an instrument, and knows how much further he wants to go in his artistic activities . . .	26	25	26
50	. . . knows how to use the arts, such as literature, drama, film, etc., to help him learn . . .	24	21	18
51	. . . develops an understanding of the plant and animals worlds, and appreciates their beauty . . .	22	21	20
52	. . . understands how he has benefitted from the cultures and heritages of other people . . .	20	21	14
53	. . . knows about the major ethical and social values of past and present cultures . . .	19	20	12
55	. . . knows about the major achievements and contributions of past civilizations . . .	18	16	11
60	. . . keeps informed about artistic activities in the community so that he can enjoy them . . .	8	8	8

considered the last goal as "very important." Listed for each of the goals is the percentage of parents, teachers, and students (of Junior and Senior high school age) who thought each was very important.

Considering the amount of intermittent public discussion about the failure of schools to teach the basic skills of reading, writing, and arithmetic, it may seem surprising that this goal was not placed first. But, the timing of public responses is important; the Massachusetts survey was completed shortly after the Watergate scandal, and the country was deeply concerned about the morality of public officials. More recently, public concern has swung back to the basic academic skills, and there is now a good deal of pressure on the schools to insist on such policies as high school graduation competency tests and promotion from one grade to another only after students have demonstrated achievement of grade goals. In a broader national study in 1976, as Figure 4 indicates, a concern for the

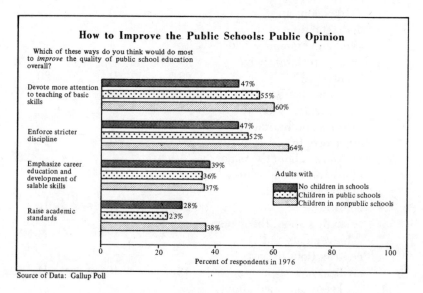

Source of Data: Gallup Poll

Figure 4.

Source: Reprinted from *The Conditions of Education 1977*, U.S. Department of Health, Education, and Welfare, p. 21.

teaching of basic skills was one of the two major recommendations of the respondents.

Notice, in Table 2,, how close the two groups of adults are in the degree of importance they give to various goals, and how far they sometimes are from the views of the students. But despite these differences, in very general terms the students agree with the adults on the ranking, so teachers can generally depend on a great deal of support for what they are trying to do.

Notice, also, how many of the goals that are thought to be important have to do with "attitude," "character," or "personality," rather than with clearcut skills or unarguable subject matter. The two on the very top of the list are obviously very difficult educational aims to impart, and some might think that they are really the province of the parent, the minister, or the psychologist. But we have always taken for granted that teachers have a part in these character-building influences on children.

Many of the problems teachers face involve school aims of this kind. It is one thing to say that children should have the confidence to do what is right, but how are they to know what *is* right? Some of the new "values" materials used in many schools attempt to persuade teachers to keep their own values —and their own ideas of what is right or wrong—out of the picture, and to guide students to develop their own values. Some teachers and parents agree with that approach, others do not.

Suppose, for instance, that a small child comes into the classroom and tells the teacher that he had bought a piece of candy that morning, and just discovered that, in the change, the clerk had mistakenly given him a dime instead of a penny. Most teachers would suggest that it is dishonest to keep the fruits of the mistake, but how are they to explain *why*? The new values curriculum would suggest the following dialogue, with the teacher playing a guidance role:[4]

> Miss Wright: Had you thought about the clerk?
> Johnny: He's dumb, not to be able to tell a dime from a penny.
> Miss Wright: Did you know you had a dime when you picked it up?

Johnny: No, I thought I had four cents until I got upstairs.

Miss Wright: Then, at first glance, you couldn't tell the difference?

Johnny: Well, if I'd looked closely, I could.

Miss Wright: Did the clerk look closely?

Johnny: Well, I guess we can all make mistakes.

Miss Wright: If you had made the mistake, how would you feel about it?

Johnny: I suppose I'd be sorry. . . .

Miss Wright: If the clerk had given you a ten-dollar bill instead of a one, what would you have done?

Johnny: Oh, I'd take it right back. I wouldn't want him to lose nine dollars.

Miss Wright: But it's all right for him to lose nine cents?

Johnny: That's not much money.

Miss Wright: How much money would it have to be before you thought you ought to take it back?

Johnny: I don't know. I hadn't thought about it that way. Do you think I ought to take back the dime?

Miss Wright: What do *you* think, Johnny?

But many teachers might, instead, take the opportunity to teach an ethical idea directly, as in this possible dialogue:

Miss Williams: The dime doesn't belong to you. You did not earn it and your father didn't give it to you.

Johnny: No, but the man at the candy store did.

Miss Williams: He thought it was a penny.

Johnny: But what difference does it make?

Miss Williams: When he counts the day's receipts, he will be short nine cents. The owner of the store will make the clerk pay it. Perhaps the clerk has a little boy. Would you want that other boy to go without his candy?

Johnny: His father should be more careful.

Miss Williams: Perhaps. Nevertheless, if all business were run on the basis of keep-what-you-get, whether it is fair or not, our whole country would be in serious trouble.

Johnny: But what difference would two candy bars make to the whole country?

Miss Williams: It isn't just the two candy bars. It isn't fair for you to profit by the clerk's error. The principle of fair play is important to all of us.

Still other teachers would handle it by emphasizing the legal question, or that of property rights, or personal integrity, or

142

they might simply rely on authority—"I say it's wrong." In any event, it is clear that a simply stated educational aim may present a very complicated dilemma for the teachers who must carry it out in the practical settings of the school.

Indeed, in the real world of the school, and particularly at the secondary level, the behavior of some groups of students has become so difficult for schools to deal with that ethical questions must take second place to what some teachers see as the sheer need to survive. It is to these problems that we now turn.

Behavior Disorders in the Schools

By the late 1970s there was a growing public sense of what could be regarded as "crime and violence" in the schools of the country. In the interests of fairness, some estimate needs to be offered of the extent to which this concern should affect a decision to enter teacher training.

The problem was considered so serious that Congress asked for a study of school disorders nationally, and a number of separate studies were also funded, so there is a good deal known about what is actually happening. First, strictly from the point of view of teachers:

1. Within the classroom itself, teachers report about one out of every five students presenting some discipline problem or behavior disorder.[5] But they rate the majority of these disorders as mild, and only a small number as severe. Teachers see a gradual rise in such behavior from kindergarten to grad five, then a decrease between grades six and twelve, possi because many disturbed youngsters drop out of high s early. Disorders among boys are reported higher than girls by a two-to-one ratio.

2. About one of ten teachers have something st them each month; the value is generally below $ of one percent a month report some kind of as person. One of five of these incidents require ment. The rates for secondary teachers are: one chance in eight of having something st

143

being robbed, one in 200 of being attacked.[6] Unlike the more usual classroom discipline problems, this behavior is much more common in the high schools than in the elementary schools.

Though these figures are likely to put people off, they must be interpreted in the light of a number of related considerations.

1. These are national averages, and the chance of these events occurring vary dramatically from one type of school district to another. Elementary school teachers in a small suburban or rural district are not at risk to the same extent as high school teachers in the slums of a major city.

2. Most of the school problems that worry the public and the school staffs do not involve teachers directly. Violent encounters of one kind or another, as well as stealing, are much more likely to occur between students; school vandalism (running at about $200 million a year) directly affects neither teachers nor students though it may reduce the pleasantness of the environment for everyone.

3. Incidents of this sort have never been uncommon in many U.S. schools, and it is possible that the difference between the past and the present is that there is a good deal more public attention being paid now to disorders in the schools. A 1974 survey of discipline problems in Georgia secondary schools, for instance, compared its findings with a similar study in 1961 and found some increase in the percentage of principals reporting the presence of a few types of problems, but not much change overall. One major difference was the use of narcotics: none was reported in 1961, but 24 percent of the principals reported it in 1974, along with 12 percent who mentioned that selling narcotics was a common misbehavior and 13 percent who said that possession of narcotics was common. (It should be noted that much of this traffic is in marijuana.) But the five most common types of misbehavior in the 1974 survey were truancy, failure to do homework and other assignments, impertinence and discourtesy to teachers and administrators, using obscene and profane language, and smoking on school grounds. With the exception of profanity, all these had been listed among the five most common problems in the earlier decade. Physical vio-

144

lence against teachers and other staff, by the way, was reported as common by less than one-half of one percent of the principals. The writers end their report of the study with the remark: "Behavior in the school seems to reflect the behavior of individuals in society as a whole. A comparison of the two surveys indicates an increase in disrespect for authority, increased use of profane or obscene language, more frequently of a serious nature, and increased use of drugs. Is this not true of the nation as a whole?"[7]

Public Attitudes

Despite all this, the consumers of schooling—parents and students—fairly consistently offer positive answers to questions that probe their attitudes about schools. The Gallup Organization surveyed public opinion about education in a series of recent polls, and in answer to the question, "In what ways are the local public schools particularly good?" respondents mentioned the following, listed in the order of the number of mentions:

1. curriculum
2. teachers
3. school facilities
4. extracurricular activities
5. up-to-date teaching methods
6. absence of racial conflicts
7. good administration

Teachers can certainly take pride in their position on that list of what the public sees as good about the schools. Furthermore, over 40 percent of parents of public school children report that their overall attitude toward the schools has become more favorable in recent years (as against 30 percent whose opinion has not changed, and a similar percentage who report a change for the worse). In this chapter we have reproduced a chart (Figure 5) comparing public confidence in education with its confidence in other institutions in society, showing that education enjoys a greater degree of public confidence than do most other institutions.

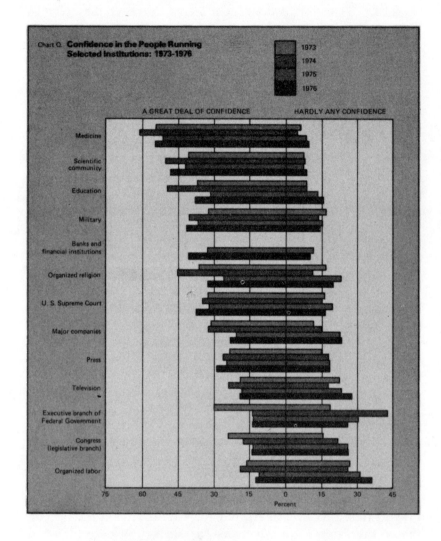

Figure 5.

Source: Reprinted from *Social Indicators 1976,* U.S. Department of Commerce, p. xlvii.

Students are, of course, closest of all to the daily life of schools. A recent survey of leading high school juniors and seniors provided the following mixed, but mostly positive, results:[8]

> 39 percent viewed their years of schooling as "challenging," 84 percent as "important," though 58 percent said it was "routine."
>
> 73 percent thought their high school subjects relevant, 20 percent said they were irrelevant.
>
> On teachers: 38 percent rated them "adequate," 55 percent "good," and only 3 percent "poor."
>
> School was in general "stimulating" for 54 percent, boring for only 37 percent.
>
> 72 percent felt their school was concerned about their overall welfare; only 22 percent felt that it was not.
>
> Only 7 percent thought their schools were "dangerous"; 86 percent listed them as "safe."

In the face of problems that the schools confront and the public pressures under which they must work, this is not a bad report card.

NOTES

[1] Based on Seymour B. Sarason, et al., *The Preparation of Teachers* (New York: John Wiley & Sons, 1962), pp. 39–52.

[2] "Time Devoted to School Duties," *NEA Research Bulletin,* vol. 40 (October 1962).

[3] *Public Response to Educational Goals, 1974–75,* Massachusetts Educational Assessment Program, State Department of Education (May 1975).

[4] *Moral and Spiritual Values in the Public Schools,* Educational Policies Commission, National Education Association (1951) pp. 37–45.

[5] Thomas J. Kelly, L. M. Bullock, and M. Kay Dykes, "Behavior Disorders: Teacher Perceptions," *Exceptional Children,* February 1977, pp. 316–18.

[6] U. S., Dept. of Health, Education, and Welfare, *Violent Schools-Safe Schools* (Washington, D.C., December 1977).

[7] Albert J. Kingston and Harold W. Gentry, "Discipline Problems in Georgia Secondary Schools—1961 and 1974," *NASSP Bulletin,* February 1977, p. 99.

[8] D. D. Miller, "What Do High School Students Think of Their Schools?" *Phi Delta Kappa,* June 1976, p. 700.

10

Teacher Preparation for Non-School Jobs

The uncertainties of the professional job market suggest that it is wise to choose an area of training at the undergraduate level that will apply as much as possible to more than one job opportunity. Training as a teacher, particularly if it is supplemented by a few years of actual experience in the classroom, provides an excellent background for a wide variety of positions in private industry as well as in government. This chapter lists a number of those positions that might be attractive to students interested in working at something related to teaching skills, but not necessarily in the school classroom. The possibilities should also be of interest to those who intend to prepare for a teaching career; one cannot predict what circumstances may later arise that make it necessary or desirable to change careers.

Teaching-Related Careers

Textbook salesperson. Elementary and high school textbook publishing is a large business, and companies perennially have many positions available for full-time salespeople. Most of them require a good deal of traveling and hence appeal to single persons, but many married men and women are willing to take on some regional travel. Some of these jobs involve doing teaching demonstrations, using the materials of the publisher one represents; others require meeting with school principals, superintendents, curriculum committees, and state department of education personnel. Publishers of college textbooks also use travelers to call on professors and college bookstores. This position requires you to be on the lookout for possible texts to publish, and can lead to a wide range of textbook editorial jobs.

Recreation Worker. Anyone with teaching skills who is good at sports might find this an interesting occupation. Federal and state park services employ a wide variety of workers in this field, and local civic organizations, public and private, such as YMCA's, use many recreation supervisors in programs for older people, members of health clubs, etc. There are about one hundred thousand part-time positions available during the summer, so those interested can find out what the occupation is like without too much trouble. (For details on where to write for specifics, see McKee's book cited at the end of this chapter.) Among the specific jobs within the field are administrators and and assistants, arts and crafts specialists, and play therapists.

Youth Organization Workers. Many national organizations devoted to youth activities (such as Boy Scouts of America, 4-H Clubs, and Campfire Girls) hire people with teaching training and experience to take over a number of administrative, supervisory, and educational tasks that must be done on a local and national level.

Customer Service Representatives. A great many private companies hire people to carry out tasks that are essentially instructional for their customers, as part of the package of goods and services the companies sell. Utilities such as telephone and electric service industries hire many such people to train their customers in the use of new equipment or to improve the effectiveness of old equipment. Cosmetic companies train beauty operators to use their products, appliance manufacturers have similar services, and most large companies hire at least a small number of people for jobs of this kind.

Technical Writers. This is a particularly appropriate job for those with teacher training and experience, because most such positions involve instructional skills. The jobs occur in a wide variety of fields: on any one of the numerous trade publications, professional journals, or newspapers, and with textbook publishers (in an editorial capacity); in industry, writing operating manuals and preparing proposals and publicity releases; with government bureaus, including the armed forces, writing bulletins and manuals; with advertising agencies having technical accounts (for example, agencies whose job it is to develop ads for pharmaceutical companies that communicate with the medical field).

College Administrative Officers. This career line offers a great variety of positions, including work in the registrar or admissions office, the office of research administration, institutional research, etc. One of these fields particularly close to teaching is that of placement—the college office that works with young people as they move into the world of work. A person in this position keeps in touch with potential employers, keeps up with the state of the employment field generally, interviews students and counsels them, and talks with field recruiters sent on campus by various firms looking for new personnel.

Organization Executive Secretary. There are thousands of trade and professional associations in the U.S., all of them with central offices and a variety of people to run them. The administrative chief is usually called the executive secretary, and is in charge of all the association's activities—arranging meetings, lobbying for the organization before public bodies of many kinds, collecting dues, handling promotion, and doing many other duties. Many associations are small and require little in the way of management; other larger ones have very sizeable staffs and need many specialists.

Religious Educator. All of the major churches use teachers in a number of positions—in direct instructional tasks in religious education, to work with volunteers, with community groups, and to produce musical programs. College degrees are given in this specialty of the educational field, but many positions are open to nonspecialists with some teaching background or training.

Red Cross Field Representatives. The Red Cross hires several different kinds of technical field representatives. One of these positions requires working with Red Cross youth programs, setting them up in the schools in cooperation with students and administrators.

Magazine Editorial Worker. The glamorous national magazines are not easy to break into, but there are thousands of specialized journals that hire editorial workers. Trade and professional journals are only one variety; there are also house organs—magazines produced within a company either for employees or for both employees and customers; there are special-interest journals aimed at a great variety of consumers and collectors who need to be kept informed and in touch with one another.

VISTA Volunteer. VISTA (Volunteers in Service to America) is the domestic counterpart of the Peace Corps (described later in this chapter). The aim of the two organizations is the same: to assist those in need. VISTA teacher-volunteers provide service in both formal classrooms and community settings, on Indian reservations and in city slums, to old and young. A typical assignment is to help with basic instruction for illiterate older persons. There are no specific educational requirements for volunteers, although teaching experience is desirable. Volunteers are provided with a six-week training period, and sign up for a year's service, which can be extended.

Careers for Specialized Teachers

Science teachers. Those prepared to teach one of the sciences start out with at least an A.B. in one of the major fields, and may be in a position to get beginning jobs in their particular scientific areas (biology, chemistry, or physics) in industry or in government. A person majoring in mathematics, with some special work in statistics, may qualify for a job as a statistician, or in one of the computer specializations.

Agriculture. There are jobs in the U.S. Cooperative Extension Service, for those with this specialization. Jobs in this field can also be found in private industry (rural area banks, for example) and in some advertising agencies and agricultural publications.

Home Economics. Increasing opportunities are available for trained people in this field. Many large companies need to staff consumer information and consumer relations departments, and that need is growing steadily with national interest in consumerism. Teachers of home economics who have good writing skills can find jobs in the field of publications and communications generally, and in the publicity departments of industries that are in the business of supplying the home.

Business Education. Teachers in this field are usually aware of the many opportunities available to people with business skills. Two-year community-college programs often have upper-level teaching opportunities in this area, and the two-year community college is the only type of higher education institution that is still expanding. The federal government is investing increased resources in manpower training programs, many of which can utilize the skills of the business educator. Teachers in this field often move into the private sector, where there is a consistent need for good supervisors.

Physical Education. Many teachers in this field set up their own summer camps, or work for such organizations. Other career possibilities include promotional jobs with sporting equipment manufacturers, and with the growing network of health clubs in the larger cities.

Reading specialists. Teacher training programs provide some specialized skills in reading instruction, and it is relatively easy to find programs in which that specialty is given major attention. In most cities one can now find private reading clinics, some for children who need special assistance and others for adults who want to increase their reading speed and comprehension. All such clinics provide some early training in the use of their own techniques, but general skills and knowledge in the area of reading instruction are very advantageous.

Government Careers

One out of every six persons in the civilian labor force works for the government at some level, from the municipalities to the federal agencies, with teachers and other persons in education making up about a third of those workers. The second largest group of government workers are in defense agencies. The rest do every imaginable kind of work.

There is a sizeable amount of turnover in this diverse work force, with about seventy thousand jobs a year opening up. And the actual size of the work force is steadily growing at a much faster rate in state and local governments than in federal agencies. Salaries have been made competitive with private industry for the most part, and fringe benefits, at the federal level particularly, are excellent.

Despite a good deal of public resistance to the growth of government, and to the taxes that must be paid for it, government jobs will probably continue to grow in the 1980s. The demand for services is just as great as the resistance to taxes, and most manpower experts agree that a possible slowdown in the rate of growth is all that can be expected. The increase in regulation by federal government agencies, among other factors, will no doubt lead to slow but steady growth.

Interagency boards run by the U.S. Civil Service Commission are located throughout the country; they disseminate information about civil service examinations, conduct the examinations themselves, and refer applicants to specific agencies. Passing the Federal Service Entrance Examination makes one eligible for over two hundred occupations throughout the country, but applicants may also directly contact agencies for which they are interested in working. For information about procedures, write to the U.S. Civil Service Commission, Washington, D.C., 20415; you will be sent the booklet *Federal Service Entrance Examination*.

The following general occupational categories are among the most important in various federal agencies:

> *Investigator*. Illustrative agencies: Veterans Administration, Department of Labor, Civil Service Commission.
> *Narcotics agent*. Department of Justice.
> *Customs inspector*. U.S. Customs.
> *Management analyst*. Employed by all large agencies.
> *Computer specialist*. Government is the largest user of computers, and every department needs these specialists.

Social service representative. Social Security Administration.

Personnel specialists. All departments.

Administrative officer. All departments.

Budget specialist. All departments.

Claims examiners. Department of Health, Education and Welfare; Treasury Department; Civil Service Commission, etc.

Public health program specialist. U.S. Public Health Service.

Quality control specialist. NASA and many others.

Information specialist. All federal agencies.

Teaching Overseas

Instead of entering allied fields, persons prepared to teach might wish to think about broadening their experience by teaching for a year or two abroad.

The Department of Health, Education and Welfare has developed a number of exchange programs; eligibility usually requires not only a teaching license but several years of teaching experience. Such programs involve a switch between an American teacher and a teacher in a foreign country, each taking over the other's job for a year. Arrangements about salary and leave of absence vary. For information write to: Teacher Exchange Section, Division of International Exchange, Institute of International Studies, Office of Education, Washington, D.C. 20202.

The U.S. Army hires many teachers to teach in schools for the children of Army personnel stationed abroad. At least two years' recent teaching experience is required and, as one might expect, positions are available at times in some rather exotic locales, as well as in Western Europe. For information write to: Department of the Army, Deputy Chief of Staff for Personnel, Dependents School Teacher Recruitment Branch, The Pentagon, Washington, D.C. 20310.

The Peace Corps is a volunteer group of teachers and experts in vocational fields who spend two years in one of the developing countries, providing instruction in fields that will most help the country. Members of the corps generally live at the level of those villagers or townspeople whom they are there to help, and it may be a lonely two years as well. The program obviously requires a very real commitment to help the disadvantaged of the world.

Other possibilities for teaching overseas, as well as further information on careers for teachers, may be found in *New Careers for Teachers* by Bill McKee, published by Henry Regnery Company.

11

Resources

Annotated Bibliography

The bibliography that follows has been carefully selected to give the reader guidance in pursuing any of the major topics in the book. References in the books themselves will indicate other books and articles on specific issues. Some of the titles may be available in a good public library, but many of them are likely to be shelved only in a college or university library.

Theoretical and Practical Concepts

Broudy, Harry S. *The Real World of the Public Schools*. New York: Harcourt Brace Jovanovich, 1972.
A reply to the many critics of American schools. Broudy, a respected educational philosopher, makes a case for the position that our public schools, though they can be improved, are doing a reasonably good job.

Herndon, James. *The Way It Spozed To Be*. New York: Simon & Schuster, 1968.
A young teacher presents his ideas for educating black slum children, e.g., giving them a choice of what they should do in school. A blistering attack on the schools as they are.

Holt, John. *How Children Fail*. New York: Pitman Publishing, 1964.

One of the most popular of the many books of the 1960s and early 1970s that criticized the schools for their "mind-crippling" insistence that pupils do what they are told and please teachers, and which advocated giving children more freedom to determine their own education.

Maccia, Elizabeth S., et al., *Women and Education.* Springfield, Mass.: Charles C. Thomas, 1975.

An excellent collection of pieces on women's intellectual growth, sex concepts in the school, how women appear in school curricula and textbooks, and the future of feminism.

Morris, Van Cleve. *Existentialism in Education.* New York: Harper and Row, 1966.

One of a series of short books, each devoted to a significant philosophical position, written for the non-specialist. Other volumes are on pragmatism and idealism.

Neill, A. S. *Summerhill, a Radical Approach to Child Rearing.* New York: Hart Publishing, 1960.

The classic and very influential description of the philosophy and operations of Neill's school in England, where children are in charge of their own education. One of the books that did a great deal to spread the open-education ideas of the 1960s.

Rogers, Vincent R. *Teaching in the British Primary School.* New York: Macmillan, 1970.

British ideas have had a great deal of influence on the U.S. elementary school in recent years, and this book describes the origin of these ideas and practices.

Silberman, Charles. *Crisis in the Classroom.* New York: Random House, 1970.

Troost, Cornelius J., ed. *Radical School Reform, Critique and Alternatives.* Boston: Little Brown, 1973.

Answers to the "open education" advocates of the 1960s and early 1970s. This should be read in tandem with Silberman.

Textbooks for Teacher Training

Blake, Kathryn A. *The Mentally Retarded, An Educational Psychology.* Englewood Cliffs, N.J.: Prentice-Hall, 1976.

A careful review of the field of mental retardation and the experience of being a teacher in this field.

Cooper, James M., et al. *Classroom Teaching Skills: A Handbook*. Lexington, Mass.: D.C. Heath, 1977.

A modern text based on the "teacher competency" approach, with careful attention to very specific teaching skills. An accompanying workbook is also available.

Cronbach, Lee J., *Educational Psychology*, 3d. ed. New York: Harcourt Brace Jovanovich, 1977.

One of the standard texts in psychological foundations, written by one of the most respected educational psychologists in the field.

Cuban, Larry. *To Make A Difference: Teaching in the Inner City*. New York: Free Press, 1970.

A description of the problems faced by teachers in urban slum schools, by a teacher with fourteen years of experience. Out of that experience Cuban has developed an organized approach to teaching poor minority youngsters.

Crystal, John C. and Richard N. Bolles. *Where Do I Go From Here with My Life?* New York: Seabury Press, 1974.

A workbook for vocational counselling. A good example of the kind of textbook material that involves the reader in activities instead of simply providing information.

Froschl, Merle, and Jane Williamson. *Feminist Resources for Schools and Colleges: A Guide to Curricular Materials*. Feminist Press, 1977.

A comprehensive annotated bibliography of nonsexist books, pamphlets, articles, and other materials for teachers and students.

Grambs, Jean D., John C. Carr, and Robert M. Fitch. *Modern Methods in Secondary Education*, Third Edition (New York: Holt, Rinehart and Winston, 1970).

An example of a text used in secondary sequences, one with a humanist orientation to teaching.

Ianni, Francis A. J., ed. *Conflict and Change in Education*. Glenview, Ill.: Scott, Foresman, 1975.

One of the better anthologies on the social foundations, made up of reprinted selections from the most recent literature. Major section headings: Social Values, Changing Lives Through Education, Education and Equalizing Opportunity, Education as a Profession, Education and the Community, Education and Social Policy.

Kohl, Herbert. *Reading, How to*. New York: Bantam, 1974.

Addressed to a popular audience, this book treats reading as something anyone can teach. It is rich in practical descriptions of how children learn to read.

Lindgren, Henry C. *Educational Psychology in the Classroom*. 4th ed. New York: John Wiley & Sons, 1972.

A good example of a widely used psychological foundation text, with a more than usual focus on application of theory to classroom situations.

Ornstein, Allan C. *An Introduction to the Foundations of Education*. Chicago: Rand McNally, 1977.

A popular introduction representing those books that are texts rather than collections of articles. Good coverage of historical and philosophical foundations in addition to its primary emphasis on the social.

Ozmon, Howard, and Sam Craver. *Philosophical Foundations of Education*. Columbus, Ohio: Charles E. Merrill, 1975.

A representative text in philosophical foundations, describing in separate sections major schools of thought in education: idealism, realism, pragmatism, reconstructionism, behaviorism, existentialism, and analytic philosophy.

Ryan, Kevin, and James M. Cooper. *Those Who Can, Teach*. 2nd ed. Boston: Houghton, Mifflin, 1975.

A popular text for a course that many teacher-training programs offer: an introduction to teaching as a profession and as an art. This text is accompanied by a book of readings.

Trump, J. Lloyd, and Delmas F. Miller. *Secondary School Curriculum Improvement*. Boston: Allyn & Bacon, 1973.

A good overview of both junior and senior high school curriculum, and an example of a secondary school professional course textbook.

Vannier, Maryhelen, and Hollis F. Fait. *Teaching Physical Education in Secondary Schools*. 4th ed. Philadelphia: Saunders, 1975.
Representative text for physical education teachers.

Teaching and the Teaching Career

Andrews, J. D., ed. *Early Childhood Education—It's An Art. It's a Science?* Washington: National Association for the Education of Young Children, 1976.
A useful introduction to what people in the early childhood field agree on, and what they are currently arguing about.

Blum, Albert A., ed. *Teacher Unions and Associations*. Urbana, Ill.: University of Illinois Press, 1969.
A thorough review of the development of teacher associations in a book that also examines their rise in other countries.

Davdell, Dorothy and Joseph, *Your Career in Teaching*. New York: Julian Messner, 1975.

Fallon, Berlie J., ed. *40 Innovating Programs in Early Childhood Education*. Belmont, Cal.: Lear Siegler, 1973.
Excellent overview of the varieties of early childhood programs available.

Goodlad, John I., and M. Francis Klein. *Behind the Classroom Door*. Worthington, Ohio: Charles A. Jones, 1970.
A survey of some of the nation's classrooms to find out how many of the educational innovations proposed in recent years have actually been adopted. This book contains a good brief review of classroom practices.

Howes, Virgil M. *Informal Teaching in the Open Classroom*. New York: Macmillan, 1974.
A how-to-do-it book on teaching focused on a teaching style that gives a great deal of freedom to the children.

Palardy, J. Michael, ed. *Teaching Today*. New York: Macmillan, 1975.
An anthology containing a sampling of current teaching problems and arguments about teaching, drawn from recent literature.

Rubin, David. *The Rights of Teachers.* An American Civil Liberties Union Handbook. New York: Avon Books, 1972.

Describes teachers' constitutional rights, and how individual teachers can protect these rights. Covers freedom to teach, freedoms of speech, association, religion; and what to do about arbitrary and discriminatory action by school officials.

Ryan, David G. *Characteristics of Teachers.* Washington, D.C.: American Council on Education, 1960.

Probably the most elaborate research on teacher attitudes and classroom behavior ever undertaken. Occasionally technical, but worth at least flipping through.

Strickland, Rennard, et al. *Avoiding Teacher Malpractice.* New York: Hawthorn Books, 1976.

In an era in which private citizens are increasingly going into court with charges of malpractice against professionals, teachers must be aware of what care they must exercise to protect themselves against suits. This book covers a wide variety of such problems, and describes some of the major court cases involving teachers' legal responsibilities.

Life in Schools

Adams, Raymond S., and Bruce J. Biddle. *Realities of Teaching.* New York: Holt, Rinehart & Winston, 1970.

A very close and detailed study of life in the classroom; what teachers and pupils actually do, and how they interact.

Cottle, Thomas J. *The Voices of School.* Boston: Little Brown, 1973.

Long, detailed interviews with children about their educational experiences. Cottle is a "child advocate," so the reports make little attempt to analyze situations beyond reporting the child's perception.

Cusick, Philip A. *Inside High School.* New York: Holt, Rinehart & Winston, 1973.

A social scientist spent half a year inside a high school, attending classes and hanging out with the students. This is his report of what student life in school is like.

Eddy, Elizabeth. *Walk the White Line*. Garden City, N.Y.: Doubleday, 1967.

An anthropologist examines a number of city slum-school classrooms.

Flender, Harold, ed. *We Were Hooked*. New York: Random House, 1972.

Thirteen young ex-addicts tell about their experience with heroin, speed, LSD and other drugs, and how they kicked the habit. Based on interviews by Flender.

Hackett, Peter, et al. *Educational Perspectives on the Drug Crisis*. Charlottesville: University of Virginia, 1971.

A collection of articles from a number of different perspectives on how the school can help to deal with increasing drug abuse among young people.

Jackson, Philip W. *Life in Classrooms*. New York: Holt, Rinehart & Winston, 1968.

Systematic study of classroom behavior. Jackson's answer to the question of what children do in class is: They wait around.

Levine, Alan, Eve Cary and Diane Divoky. *The Rights of Students*. New York: E. P. Dutton, 1973.

The rights of students to constitutional protection is a very prominent feature of the current high school scene. This book was written primarily for students, by the American Civil Liberties Union; it spells out the rights the courts have granted, and those they have not.

Wolcott, Harry F. *The Man in the Principal's Office*. New York: Holt, Rinehart & Winston, 1973.

A detailed study of an elementary school principal, how he spends his time, deals with his teachers, what his problems are, etc.

Teacher Training

Evans, Ellis D. *Transition to Teaching*. New York: Holt, Rinehart & Winston, 1976.

Concentrates on the process of becoming a teacher, from the

preparation at the end of the training period, to the initial shock of adjusting to the first year or so on the job.

Gregory, Thomas B. *Encounters with Teaching.* Englewood Cliffs, N.J.: Prentice-Hall, 1972.

A description of and guide to micro-teaching, one of the major innovations in teacher-training technique.

Keach, Everett T., Jr. *Elementary School Student Teaching: A Casebook.* New York: John Wiley & Sons, 1966.

Twenty-two brief cases of real problems in student teaching situations.

Koerner, James D. *The Miseducation of American Teachers.* Boston: Houghton Mifflin, 1963.

This is a classic attack on teacher education that created a national stir when it was first published, and is still referred to in education literature.

National Teacher Examination. New York: Arco Publishing, 1973.

One of a Professional Career Examination Series, this volume is an aid to those preparing to take the NTE. Provides an excellent sample idea of the kinds of items that are included in such exams.

New Teachers: New Education. National Education Association, 1970.

A collection of reports from students about their experiences in innovative teacher education programs.

Peter, Laurence J. *Competencies For Teaching.* Belmont, Cal.: Wadsworth, 1975.

A simple description of the competency-based approach to teacher education.

Ryan, Kevin, ed. *Teacher Education.* The 74th Yearbook of the National Society for the Study of Education, Part 2. Chicago: University of Chicago Press, 1975.

A review of the state of teacher education by a group of university educators.

Smith, B. Othanel, Saul B. Cohen, and Arthur Pearl. *Teachers for the Real World.* American Association of Colleges for Teacher Education, 1969.

A call for change in teacher education, from a group of teacher educators primarily interested in improving the teaching of disadvantaged children, and in teaching from a humanistic perspective.

Stone, James C. *Breakthrough in Teacher Education.* San Francisco: Jossey-Bass, 1968.

Description and evaluation of a number of innovative teacher education programs funded by the Ford Foundation Breakthrough Project.

Universities with Innovative Teacher Training Programs

A considerable number of teacher training programs have experimented with innovative training ideas in the past decade or so. The list below does not pretend to be complete in any sense, but it does include those institutions that either had received special grants from the Ford Foundation, or had been singled out by the U.S. Office of Education as developers of new models of teacher training. The special program that prompted selection for this list may or may not still be functioning, however, and interested students should write to the specific school of education requesting a current catalog.

Antioch College	Syracuse University
Ball State University	University of Georgia
Brigham Young University	University of Massachusetts
Columbia University,	University of Pittsburgh
Teachers College	University of Toledo
Florida State University	University of Washington
Michigan State University	University of Wisconsin-
New Mexico State University	Milwaukee
San Francisco State College	Wayne State University

Components of Teacher Training Programs

The following tables showing the status of a number of aspects of teacher training college curricula are reproduced

Total Number of Hours Required in Professional Education
(N=440)

	Elementary Teaching		Secondary Teaching	
	No.	%	No.	%
15 hours or less	6	1%	23	5%
16-25 hours	81	18%	336	76%
26-35 hours	202	46%	52	12%
36-45 hours	85	19%	8	2%
46-55 hours	20	5%	1	.2%
56-65+ hours	10	2%	3	.7%
NA	36	8%	17	4%
Totals	440	99%	440	99.9%

Figure 6.

Number of Course Hours Required in Curriculum and Instructional Methods
(N=440)

	Elementary Teaching		Secondary Teaching	
	No.	%	No.	%
10 hours or less	90	21%	315	72%
11-15 hours	129	29%	70	16%
16+ hours	176	40%	23	5%
NA	45	10%	32	7%

Figure 7.

Course Hours Required in Field Experiences
(N=440)

	Elementary Teaching		Secondary Teaching	
	No.	%	No.	%
3 hours	21	5%	26	6%
4-6 hours	75	17%	115	26%
7-9 hours	133	30%	164	37%
10-14 hours	104	24%	75	17%
15+ hours	59	13%	33	8%
NA	48	11%	27	6%

Figure 8.

To what extent are the following used in the Professional Education sequence of courses?	Not at all %	Rarely %	Moderately %	A Great Deal %	N.A. %
Computer Assisted Instruction	54%	27%	8%	.3%	10%
Individualized Instruction	1%	11%	62%	22%	4%
Interaction Analysis	8%	30%	46%	9%	6%
Lectures	4%	7%	52%	37%	3%
Microteaching	3%	19%	54%	22%	3%
Modules and Minicourses	11%	31%	39%	13%	6%
Seminars	1%	11%	56%	30%	3%
Simulation	3%	31%	53%	8%	5%
Videotapes of student teachers	6%	18%	50%	23%	4%

Figure 9.

Field Experiences Offered by the Institution (N=719)	Freshman Year %	Sophomore Year %	Junior Year %	Senior Year %
Experience				
Student Teaching	0%	.4%	7%	97%
Classroom Observation	16%	58%	74%	31%
Tutoring	15%	46%	61%	22%
Teacher-aide experience	12%	48%	57%	15%
Community experiences (social work, clubs, etc.)	23%	42%	41%	21%
Interviews	4%	25%	44%	26%
Other	2%	2%	5%	3%

Figure 10.

167

Specialized Programs Offered by Respondents						
Program	Currently Offered		Planning to Offer		N.A.	
	No.	%	No.	%	No.	%
Open Classroom	292	41%	74	10%	353	49%
Urban Education	247	34%	44	6%	428	60%
Bilingual Education	97	14%	74	10%	548	76%
Learning Disabilities	348	48%	126	18%	245	34%
Education of the Disadvantaged	271	38%	42	6%	406	57%
Early Childhood	445	62%	98	14%	176	25%
Other programs with special needs	125	17%	24	3%	569	79%

Figure 11.

Criteria Used for Graduation From
Teacher Education Programs

	No. of Inst.	%
Minimum number of hours	696	97%
Minimum overall GPA*	658	92%
Minimum GPA in education sequence	444	62%
Minimum performance in student teaching	625	87%
Minicourse evaluations	31	4%
National Standardized Tests	89	12%
Supervisors' evaluations	517	72%
Observation Schedule analyses	115	16%
Criterion-referenced tests (locally derived)	37	5%

Figure 12.

* GPA is Grade Point Average.

Tables from: Susan S. Sherwin, *Teacher Education: A Status Report.* Copyright © 1974 by Educational Testing Service, Princeton, New Jersey. Reprinted by permission.

168

from a survey conducted jointly by Educational Testing Service and the Association of Colleges of Teacher Education. The percentages are based on a better than 80 percent return of questionnaires sent to all members of the association, which numbered nearly nine hundred colleges and universities, in 1974. A copy of the complete report is available from ETS, in Princeton, New Jersey, under the title, *Teacher Education: A Status Report.*

Teacher's License Requirements

The table of minimum requirements for teacher certification in the various states is reproduced from T.M. Stinnett's *A Manual on Standards Affecting School Personnel in the U.S.* published by the National Education Association, Washington, D.C. 1974. The book contains a wealth of information on each state, including lists of accredited institutions.

Figure 13.—MINIMUM REQUIREMENTS FOR LOWEST REGULAR TEACHING CERTIFICATES*

State	Elementary School					Secondary School				
	Degree	General Education (Semester Hours)	Professional Education (Total Semester Hours)	Student Teaching (Included in Col. 4)	Educational Philosophy-Psychology-Sociology (Included in Col. 4)	Degree	General Education (Semester Hours)	Professional Education (Total Semester Hours)	Student Teaching (Included in Col. 9)	Educational Philosophy-Psychology-Sociology (Included in Col. 9)
1	2	3	4	5	6	7	8	9	10	11
Alabama	B	59	27	6	—	B	44	21	6	—
Alaska	B	AC	AC	AC	AC	B	AC	AC	AC	AC
Arizona	B[a]	40	24	6	3	B[a]	40	22	6	3
Arkansas	B	48	18	6	3	B	48	18	6	3
California	B[b]	AC	AC[†]	AC[†]	AC[†]	B[b]	AC	AC[†]	AC[†]	AC[†]
Colorado	B	AC	AC	AC	AC	B	AC	AC	AC	AC
Connecticut	B[c]	75	30	6	6	B[c]	45	18	6	6
Delaware	B	60	30	6	6	B	60	18	6	9
District of Col.	B[d]	AC	AC	AC	AC	M[d]	AC	AC	AC	AC
Florida	B	45	20	6	6	B	45	20	6	6
Georgia	B[e]	40	18	6	—	B[e]	40	18	6	—
Hawaii	B	AC	18	AC[†]	6[f]	B	AC	18	AC[†]	6[f]
Idaho	B	42	24	6	2	B	42	20	6	2
Illinois	B	78	16	5	2	B	50	16	5	6
Indiana	B[h]	97	27	8	10	B[a]	40	18	6	6
Iowa	B	40	20	5	—	B	50	20	5	—
Kansas	B	50	24	5	12	B	50	20	5	12
Kentucky	B[i]	45	24	8	—	B[i]	45	17	8	—
Louisiana	B	46	24	4	9	B	46	18	4	9
Maine	B	60	30	6	3	B	60	18	6	3
Maryland	B[k]	80	26	8	6	B[k]	—	18	6	6
Massachusetts	B[l]	—	18	2[m]	—	B[l]	—	12	2[m]	—
Michigan	B[n]	40	20	6	6[o]	B[n]	40	20	6	6[o]
Minnesota	B	AC	AC	AC	AC	B	48	27[p]	6[p]	—
Mississippi	B	48	36	6	6	B	48	18	6	6
Missouri	B	AC	18	5	7	B	40	18	5	7

State	Elementary School					Secondary School				
	Degree	General Education (Semester Hours)	Professional Education (Total Semester Hours)	Student Teaching (Included in Col. 4)	Educational Philosophy-Psychology-Sociology (Included in Col. 4)	Degree	General Education (Semester Hours)	Professional Education (Total Semester Hours)	Student Teaching (Included in Col. 9)	Educational Philosophy-Psychology-Sociology (Included in Col. 9)
1	2	3	4	5	6	7	8	9	10	11
Montana	B	AC	AC	AC	AC	B	AC	16	AC	AC
Nebraska	B[q]	AC	AC	AC	AC	B	AC	AC	AC	AC
Nevada	B	—	18[r]	6	—	B	—	20	6	—
New Hampshire	B[s]	AC	AC	AC	AC	B[s]	AC	AC	AC	AC
New Jersey	B	45	24	—[t]	—[u]	B	45	15	—[t]	—[u]
New Mexico	B	48	24	6	—	B[v]	48	18	6	—
New York	B[w]	NS	24	NS[f]	—	B[w]	NS	12	NS[f]	—
North Carolina	B	35-40%	15-20%	—	—	B	35-40%	15-20%	—	—
North Dakota	B[x]	NCATE	16	5	—	B	NCATE	16	5	—
Ohio	B	60	29	6	6	B[x]	30	21	6	6
Oklahoma	B	50	21	9	—	B	50	21	9	—
Oregon	B	—	24	6	—	B[y]	—	20	6	—
Pennsylvania	B[s]	AC	AC	AC	AC	B[s]	AC	AC	AC	AC
Rhode Island	B[aa]	42-45	30	6	3	B[aa]	42-45	18	6	3
South Carolina	B	30	21	6	—	B	42-45	18	6	—
South Dakota	B[bb]	40	26	6	—	B	—	20	6	3
Tennessee	B	40	24	4	—	B	40	24	4	—
Texas	B	60	18	6	—	B	60	18	6	—
Utah	B	AC	25	8	6	B	AC	21	8	6
Vermont	B	AC	18	9	3	B	AC	18	9	3
Virginia	B	60	18	6	3	B	48	15	6	3
Washington	B[ee]	70%[dd]	20%[dd]	—	—	B[ee]	70%[dd]	20%[dd]	—	—
West Virginia	B	40	20	6	AC	B	40	20	6	—
Wisconsin	B	AC	26	5	AC	B	AC	18	5	AC
Wyoming	B	40	23	C	—	B	40	20	C	—

LEGEND: — means not reported. AC means approved curriculum; B means completion of the bachelor's degree; M means completion of the master's degree; C means a course; NS means not specified; NCATE means standards of the National Council for Accreditation of Teacher Education.

* Requirements listed are those which are basic for lowest regular certificates. Some variations may be found in the requirements for specific certificates listed for the respective states in chapter 2.

ᵃ For the temporary certificate, valid for six years only. Teachers must qualify for the standard certificate by completing a fifth year of preparation.

ᵇ For the initial standard credential. Teachers must qualify for the permanent credential by completing a planned fifth year program of 30 semester hours (s.h.) postbaccalaureate work (or whatever constitutes a year of work in the preparing institution)—within seven years for elementary teachers, five years for secondary teachers.

† For elementary teachers, California standards apparently call for 20 s.h. of professional studies (8 student teaching, 8 educational psychology/sociology/philosophy, 4 curriculum and methods); for secondary teachers 15 s.h. (6, 6, and 3).

ᶜ For the provisional certificate, valid for five years and renewable once for five years. Teachers must qualify for the standard certificate by completing a fifth year of preparation.

ᵈ Bachelor's degree for elementary and junior high schools; master's degree for senior and vocational high schools.

ᵉ Effective July 1, 1974, the initial certificate, based on the bachelor's degree, will be nonrenewable; completion of a fifth year of preparation will be required for continuing certification.

ᶠ Not included in total professional education.

ᵍ Three s.h. in educational psychology, 3 in principles of education.

ʰ For the provisional certificate, valid for five years only; teachers must qualify for the professional certificate by obtaining a master's degree.

ⁱ For the provisional certificate, valid for ten years and extendable only on completion of a fifth year of preparation. A master's degree is required for the standard certificate.

ʲ Recommended but not required.

ᵏ For the initial certificate, valid three years and renewable for seven; teachers must qualify for the professional certificate, based on the master's degree or equivalent, after ten years of service.

ˡ Or graduation from a four-year normal school approved by the State Board of Education.

ᵐ The requirement is 6 s.h. for the bilingual education certificate.

ⁿ For the provisional certificate, valid for six years and renewable for three; teachers must complete an additional 18 s.h. for continuing certification.

ᵒ Or equivalent.

ᵖ Quarter hours.

ᑫ Elementary teachers in accredited schools must hold a certificate based on the degree. Nebraska does issue provisional rural elementary and commitment certificates on a minimum of 60 s.h., valid only for specifically endorsed grades or subjects in designated classes of school districts for a limited time.

ʳ For the five-year nonrenewable certificate; teachers must qualify for the regular certificate, which requires 30 s.h.

ˢ A provisional conversion license may be issued to the holder of a bachelor's degree from a regionally accredited institution but not in a program approved by New Hampshire. A certificate will be issued on completion of the conversion program and recommendation of the superintendent attesting to competent performance and satisfactory professional growth.

ᵗ College requirement; not included in total professional education column.

ᵘ Educational psychology, included in total professional education.

ᵛ For the provisional certificate, valid for four years and renewable once for four years. Teachers must complete a fifth year of preparation for continuing certification.

ʷ For the provisional certificate, valid for five years only. Teachers must qualify for permanent certification by completing a fifth year of preparation.

ˣ Total s.h.—124.

ʸ For the initial certificate, valid for three years and renewable once for three years. Secondary teachers must complete a fifth year of preparation for continuing certification.

ᶻ For the provisional certificate, valid for three years and renewable once for three years. Teachers must qualify for the permanent certificate by completing 24 s.h. of postbaccalaureate work.

ᵃᵃ For the provisional certificate, valid for six years only. Teachers must qualify for the professional certificate by completing a fifth year of preparation (36 s.h. or a master's degree).

ʰʰ South Dakota still lists a nondegree elementary certificate, valid for teaching grades K-9, except in K-12 school systems. The 1970 edition noted that this certificate was to be discontinued in 1972.

ᶜᶜ For the provisional certificate, valid for three years and renewable once for three years. Teachers must qualify for the standard certificate by completing a fifth year of preparation.

ᵈᵈ Ten percent electives.

Figure 15.

172

Sources for Statistics of the Field

The federal government now provides several sources of significant information about the state of education and the teaching profession. One of these is *The Condition of Education*, updated each year or so by the National Center for Educational Statistics, Department of Health, Education, and Welfare. *Social Indicators*, an even more elaborate volume, produced by the Department of Commerce, contains a substantial section on education.

The HEW volume is a good source for current labor market information, as is the *Standard Education Almanac*, published annually by Marquis Academic Media. For curriculum studies, specific information on teaching careers, and other such data, write to National Education Association, 1201 Sixteenth Street N.W., Washington, D.C. 20036.

Index

Index

Curriculum
   as a subject matter, 37–45
   bilingual education, 102–105
   early childhood, 93–94
   for the retarded, 98–99
   "hidden," 23
   in high schools, 60–63

D

Day care centers, 93
Department of Health, Educa-
   tion and Welfare, 155
Dewey, John, 33
Disadvantaged children, 94
Discipline, 63–65, 143–145
Discovery learning, 44
Doctorate in education (Ed.D),
   114–116
Drug abuse, 144–145

E

Early childhood education, 4,
   90–94
Ecology, 43
Elementary schools, 4, Ch. 2
   methods in, 45–54
   teacher training for, 5, 9
Emile, 90
English as a second language
   (ESL), 101
Erickson, Erik, 22
Exceptional children, 92

F

Family life education, 43, 63
Federal Service Entrance Examination, 154

Foreign languages, 62
Foundations of education
   typical assignments, 33–34
   psychological, 20–28
   social, 28–34

G

Goals of education, 137–140
Government jobs, 153–155
Graduate studies, Ch. 7, 57
Green, John, 109
Guidance counselor, 110

H

Handicapped Child Act, 95
Head Start, 91
High school, 58, 61
   graduation, 60
History of education, 29
Home economics, 62–63, 153
Human relations, 48
Humanism, 46–48

I

Industrial arts, 62
In-service training, 128–129
Internship, teaching, 72–73
Introduction to teaching, 19–20
I.Q. testing, 97–98

J

Job market, 121–122
Junior high school, 4, 56

Teaching internship, 72–73
Teaching methods
  for the retarded, 99–100
  in multi-ethnic programs, 103–104
Team teaching, 45, 58–59
Testing, 68–71
Textbooks, 34, 66–67
Thelen, Herbert, 16
Tracking, 60–61

U

U.S. Army schools, 155

U.S. Civil Service Commission, 154
U.S. Office of Education, 11

V

Values education, 141–143
Vandalism, 144
Verbal Interaction Category System, 51–52
Vocational education, 62
Vocational Education Act of 1963, 62
Volunteers in Service to America (VISTA), 152